Seasons

of the

SOUL

Seasons

of the

SOUL

Which one are you in?

Leon Drennan

 Vision Leadership Foundation

For more information about Vision Leadership Foundation, please visit: www.Vision-Leadership.com
or contact Leon Drennan at leon@vision-leadership.com

ISBN 978-0-9904033-4-0

First Edition

Printed in United States America

DEDICATION

This book is dedicated in loving memory of my mom and dad who taught me to work hard, persevere, and pursue God. Also to my children—in birth order—Scott, Allyson, and Kelsey. They bring me great joy and gave me three good reasons to persevere. Finally and most importantly, to my wife Debbie who has loved me unconditionally for thirty-eight years and who has persevered with me. She is my single greatest joy on this earth. She was the first one to know for sure that God wanted me to write this book.

Table of Contents

ACKNOWLEDGMENTS

I thank Diana Rush, my executive assistant of many years and trusted friend, who worked a full time job and helped in her spare time with formatting and graphics of my manuscript. Thanks to Jim Baker, Brian Ball, Debbie Drennan, Jim Jenkins, Ted Johnson, Louis Joseph, Mark Rainey, Gerald Stowe, and Dick Wells who read this and gave me such valuable feedback. Finally, I thank all my past colleagues, employees, peers, and associates for the fun we had together, what I learned from them, what we accomplished and, most importantly, for their friendship as they walked with me through many of these seasons.

ACKNOWLEDGMENTS

Introduction

Several years ago, God placed in my heart to write a book on leadership, *Good King Bad King*, and while I could see the reason for it, writing the book was some of the hardest work I've ever done. You can imagine my shock when my adorable wife, Debbie, cheerfully announced one day, "I know the title of your next book: *Seasons of the Soul*." I admit that I liked the title but in no way felt qualified to write on the topic.

I asked Debbie if this was just one of her good ideas or if she had really heard a word from the Lord. She thought for a minute and said, "I don't know, I'll have to pray about it."

Two weeks passed before she finally told me, "I prayed about it, and I know you're supposed to write that book." I learned a long time ago that if my wife says she has a word from the Lord, I don't need to question it. I just need to do it. So here I am, writing *Seasons of the Soul*.

I have to admit that at first I didn't understand why I should write this. My first book was on the five essentials of leadership and healthy organizations, based on biblical principles. But I didn't see the link between it and *Seasons of the Soul*, a more personal, spiritual book. I had already begun writing when God revealed the connection to me.

Everything in the natural world is simply a manifestation of what's going on in the spiritual world because the spiritual world drives the natural world. I've had periods of time when everything I was working on panned out just right. Yet I've had other times when I was working my hardest and doing everything right, but nothing would go the way I wanted it to. As I look back, I realize these were seasons. What was happening around me was driven by what was going on spiritually and what God was trying to do in me and through me at the time. Recognizing the significance of seasons in my own life revealed to me one of the important purposes of this book: to help you understand what spiritual season you are in so you know what to expect and how to respond to a season you want to stay in and how to get through a season that is difficult for you.

Having grown up on a farm, I can tell you that understanding the seasons of the year is critical. No matter how hard a farmer works, he could easily starve to death if he did things out of season. A farmer who plants in the winter would have disastrous results. Or if he tried to harvest in the spring, he would have little to show for it and would probably kill the growing plants. If he pruned during the summer, his plants and vines would likely die. It is easy to see how important it is for farmers to know the seasons so they know what work they need to be doing, and the same is true in our lives.

Just as there are seasons in the agricultural calendar, there are spiritual seasons for our souls. And if you do not know which season you're in, you will not understand what God wants to accomplish or what you're supposed to do. As a result, you might miss prosperous seasons or stay in difficult seasons much longer than you need to.

> *Blessed is the one who does not walk*
> *in step with the wicked or stand in the way*
> *that sinners take or sit in the company of mockers,*
> *but whose delight is in the law of the LORD,*
> *and who meditates on his law day and night.*
> *That person is like a tree planted by streams of water,*
> *which yields its fruit in season and whose leaf does not*
> *wither—whatever they do prospers.*
> Psalm 1:1-3

This is especially critical for leaders to be aware of. In *Good King Bad King*, I talk about the five essentials of a healthy, growing organization, and, for leaders, the lessons of that book need to be accompanied by the lessons of this book. Why? Because it's not only important to know what to do, but it's also important to know the right season to do things in.

> *There is a time for everything,*
> *and a season for every activity under the heaven.*
> Ecclesiastes 3:1

The purpose of this book is to provide perspective to help you:

- Identify the season you are in,
- Understand God's purpose for you in that season,
- Know the proper response during the season to realize God's best for your life.

It is critical that you understand one thing throughout this book: God's purposes are based on His love for you. He is always working in love no matter what season you are in. God will never leave you in a difficult season one minute longer than what is needed for your good and His glory—you can absolutely count on it. That is one of many reasons we can praise God in all seasons!

Darkness and Light

Broadly, there are two conditions of the soul: dark and light. If you're not a Christian, the truth is that you are in the Dark Season, and you will want to carefully consider this pre-conversion section. I also encourage you to read it, even if you believe you are a Christian, for two primary reasons:

1) Jesus said,

> *Many will say to me on that day,*
> *"Lord, Lord, did we not prophesy in your name*
> *and in your name drive out demons and in your name*
> *perform many miracles?" Then I will tell them plainly,*
> *"I never knew you. Away from me, you evildoers!"*
> Matthew 7:22

2) The Apostle Paul said we should test ourselves to see if we are in the faith.

> *Examine yourselves to see whether you are in the*
> *faith; test yourselves. Do you not realize that Christ*
> *Jesus is in you—unless, of course, you fail the test?*

And I trust that you will discover that
we have not failed the test.
2 Corinthians 13:5-6

I'm writing about the pre-conversion condition and its seasons so you can test yourself to see if you "are in the faith" and avoid the horrible tragedy of thinking you have a relationship with God when perhaps you actually don't. Also, if you are in the light yourself, you may have friends who are in one of these pre-conversion seasons, and I want to help you recognize how to help them trust Jesus.

INTRODUCTION
to the DARK SEASON

....

There is a way that appears to be right,
but in the end it leads to death.
Proverbs 14:12

People who live in spiritual darkness are not necessarily worse people than Christians. Christians have the blood of Christ covering their sins, while those who continue to live in darkness do not. Christians will live with God forever. Those who continue in darkness will live apart from God forever.

God is light and love. Imagine existing forever with no light and no love in your life and no hope of ever having either again.

This is the message we have heard from him
and declare to you: God is light;
in him there is no darkness at all.
1 John 1:5

Chapter 1

What does it mean to be in the dark? Generally, when we say we have been kept in the dark, we are not truly aware of everything we need to know to make good decisions.

Spiritually, when we say people are in the dark, we mean they are lost. They don't have a relationship with the living God. They have no hope of living with Him for eternity and serving a meaningful purpose in His kingdom unless something changes, and they are not free from the power or the penalty of sin in their lives.

The Lost Soul

For all have sinned and fall short of the glory of God.
Romans 3:23

The light shines in the darkness, and the darkness has not overcome it.
John 1:5

The season of lostness is one we all have in common. The Bible teaches that we are all sinful and hopelessly separated from God if left on our own. King David acknowledged that we are born sinful by nature from our mother's wombs. Scripture and experience show us that we are also sinful by choice.

Even babies and small children, before they are old enough

to make moral choices, are sinful and self-focused. At a very early age, children know how to lie, manipulate, and get their own way. They don't know they are sinning. They are just selfish.

As we grow and learn, we become aware that we are making moral choices and can choose good or evil, God or self, but Scripture teaches that we all choose self.

> *All of us have become like one who is unclean,*
> *and all our righteous acts are like filthy rags; we all*
> *shrivel up like a leaf, and like the wind our sins sweep*
> *us away.*
> Isaiah 64:6

> *We all, like sheep, have gone astray, each of us has*
> *turned to our own way; and the Lord has laid on him*
> *the iniquity of us all.*
> Isaiah 53:6

Simply stated, when people are lost, they are separated from God, our Creator. People are separated because of selfishness and sin, and none of us have any hope of making it right on our own. Left in this stage, we would all die and be eternally separated from God and all that is good. But there are conditions of the soul within this lostness that we should understand. God is available to us in each of these conditions, and we are accountable to Him for the choices we make, as clearly shown in this passage from Romans:

> *The wrath of God is being revealed from heaven*
> *against all the godlessness and wickedness of people,*

who suppress the truth by their wickedness,
since what may be known about God is plain to them,
because God has made it plain to them. For since the
creation of the world God's invisible qualities—his
eternal power and divine nature—have been clearly
seen, being understood from what has been made,
so that people are without excuse.
For although they knew God, they neither glorified
him as God nor gave thanks to him, but their thinking
became futile and their foolish hearts were darkened.
Although they claimed to be wise, they became fools.
Romans 1:18-22

Not everyone in the dark season is viewed as evil. There are the varying conditions of the young child, the religious soul, the person with the "right" affiliations, and the "good person." On the other hand, there is also the hardened and rebellious soul. I will share with you how to recognize each, what each one's response to God needs to be, and how you can help. The one thing they all have in common is that they are deceived, and the deception is progressive.

Go Deeper

1. In Scripture, demons often recognized Christ before God's own people did. Do you *know* God or just know about Him?

2. Do you consider yourself a sinner? If yes, what will you do about it?

3. Do you want a relationship with the living God? If yes, how will you pursue it?

4. List three people you know who are walking in darkness. What are you doing to lead them to the light?

*I*NNOCENCE

....

Even babies and children are inherently self-focused. I trust them into the hands of my merciful and just Savior, Jesus.

Chapter 2

King David indicated that he was born sinful. I would agree that we all are. But there is a season of innocence. Early on, our moral faculties are not developed, and we're not really conscious that we are rebelling against a holy and loving God. I trust God's grace to cover children until they are able to be conscious of the choices they are making.

There are those who would say small children are not sinful. Yet as I said earlier, I have observed that, from a very early age, children are self-centered and manipulative. They don't care that Mom and Dad have had no sleep. They cry when nothing hurts just because they want to be picked up and have their own way. They test boundaries and limits. Life is all about them. There's an "I" in the middle of "sin," and that description fits even small children quite well.

This season lasts a few years. Then children become aware of moral choices, and they become more aware of their consciences. They are aware of right and wrong. And every one of us consciously chooses wrong, as King David says. From this season of moral consciousness, they have a choice of which other season(s) they will go into.

Religious Soul

Jesus had harder words for the religious people in society than anyone else. He welcomed sinners of all kinds. But the purely religious people who had no real relationship with God were repulsive to Him.

Woe to you, teachers of the law and Pharisees, you hypocrites! You are like whitewashed tombs, which look beautiful on the outside but on the inside are full of the bones of the dead and everything unclean.
Matthew 23:27

Chapter 3

Although many people are just as lost as the rebellious and hardened person, they are not—or at least don't see themselves as—being openly rebellious against God and His plan. We will refer to these people as deceived souls, and there's more than one category here. The first we will discuss is the religious soul.

The religious soul has a prayer life, but not a healthy one. These people tend to be self-promoting, like the man in Scripture who prays that he is thankful not to be like the sinner he was looking down on. Religious souls tend to talk much and listen not at all. They do not have a real relationship and communion with God and expect answers to prayer from God based on their keeping up an agenda of religious activity.

Unfortunately, a large number of people fit this category. They are religious, consider themselves moral and ethical, and, many times, by human standards, they are. They go to church. They engage in religious activities and rituals. They feel good about themselves and their spiritual condition. Other people even agree with them.

So What's the Problem?

They have religion but no relationship with the living God. They have not been born again of the Spirit. Their relationship with God is not based on His mercy, grace, and the sacrifice of Jesus on the cross. Rather, they count on their religion to attain a right relationship with God. But Scripture teaches this is simply not possible.

> *Many will say to me on that day,*
> *"Lord, Lord, did we not prophesy in your name and*
> *in your name drive out demons and in your name*
> *perform many miracles?"*
> *Then I will tell them plainly, "I never knew you.*
> *Away from me, you evildoers!"*
> Matthew 7:22-23

Religion is about rituals. It's about activity and what we do to try to earn God's favor. A true relationship with God, though, is built on His grace and mercy—on what Jesus did on the cross to cover our sin, not what we can do to earn right standing with God. Salvation is based on Christ's work and is a work of the Spirit within us that creates a relationship with God through which we obey Him from the heart. We don't do good works to be saved. We do good works out of gratitude because "by grace we are saved." We are not saved *by* good works. We are saved *for* good works.

> *For we are God's handiwork, created in Christ Jesus*
> *to do good works, which God prepared*
> *in advance for us to do.*
> Ephesians 2:10

> *"For I know the plans I have for you," declares the*
> *Lord, "plans to prosper you and not to harm you,*

plans to give you hope and a future."
Jeremiah 29:11

Saul, who later became the Apostle Paul, is an example of the religious soul. He was a Pharisee and among the strictest of the religious leaders. He knew the Scriptures better than most people in his day and was extremely careful to practice what he thought the Scriptures taught. Yet he did not have a real relationship with God, and on the Damascus Road, Jesus asked why Saul was persecuting Him.

"Who are you, Lord?" Saul asked.
"I am Jesus, whom you are persecuting," he replied.
Acts 9:5

Saul thought his actions were pleasing to God, but they weren't. Saul was judgmental and harsh with people because he did not have the love of God in his heart. Because Saul was in the pre-conversion season of the soul, he had not been forgiven of his sins, and therefore he was not forgiving towards others.

Anyone who claims to be in the light but hates a
brother or sister is still in the darkness.
1 John 2:9

Such religious souls need to understand Ephesians 2:8-9:

For by grace you have been saved through faith.

> *And this is not your own doing; it is the gift of God,*
> *not a result of works, so that no one may boast.*

This scripture makes several important points. First, it says by grace you have been saved. And what is grace? It is God's unmerited favor, through which we do not get what we deserve. In fact, it's quite the opposite. We get something really good that we could never earn or deserve. Grace is God's free gift of forgiveness. (Mercy, by contrast, is God withholding the punishment that we do deserve.)

Second, we receive this grace through faith. Faith is trusting in something we can't see or touch:

> *Now faith is the assurance of things hoped for,*
> *the conviction of things not seen.*
> Hebrews 11:1 (ESV)

So what is it that we have faith in, or what do we trust in? Is it our good works, religious rituals, our family, or church connections? No. It's faith in Jesus Christ and His sacrifice on the cross to cover all our sins and make us right with a Holy God.

Third, we see it is not our own doing. We cannot do this for ourselves. We need Christ in order to be saved! And that salvation is a gift of God. As with any gift, you don't earn it, and you can't work for it. The only way to rightly receive a gift is simply to accept it. When we accept a gift, we have no basis for boasting in what we have been given. We have the gift because of God's grace, not because of our goodness.

How do we accept this gift? By placing faith in Jesus Christ as the Savior and Lord of our lives. This means we trust Him with our eternity and future and that we trust Him with our lives in the here and now. Having Jesus as Lord means that now He is making the decisions, and we are following His direction in all things.

> *If you declare with your mouth, "Jesus is Lord,"*
> *and believe in your heart that God raised him from*
> *the dead, you will be saved.*
> Romans 10:9

Go Deeper

1. Do you consider yourself a religious person or a spiritual person?

2. Do you care more about keeping the rules or loving people?

3. Are your prayers warm and personal or stiff?

4. Do you know Jesus on a personal basis, or do you just know about Him?

5. What in your life shows your friends the difference between being religious versus being Spirit-led?

AFFILIATED

We are a society of networkers. Networking has become a huge thing in professional circles. Some people count on their contact list more than they count on God. Having a lot of spiritual affiliations with people is good—but they won't make you right with God.

Jesus answered,
"I am the way and the truth and the life.
No one comes to the Father except through me."
John 14:6

Chapter 4

We live in a society where people get positions, perks, and privileges based on who they know. That reality is so ingrained that when I graduated from college and got a job in Nashville, one man in my rural community asked me who I knew "up there."

The question upset me because I had studied hard, earned good grades, and didn't know anybody in Nashville at the time. Perhaps I actually was an exception to the rule. But the truth is, many people have affiliations with other people that have gotten them where they are. This brings up an interesting parallel to how Jewish people in Jesus' time thought. They believed that, because they were descendants of Abraham, they were guaranteed a relationship with God.

I understand well the mindset of the religious people who think they can be good enough to earn a right standing with God through their works. After all, I got a job in Nashville because of my own hard work and grades. But when it comes to a relationship with God, that absolutely does not work. I can't earn it. You can't. Nobody can. "Our works do not empower a relationship with God. Rather, our relationship with God—once we have one—empowers our works." [1]

With God, it really is a case of who you know, but it still doesn't necessarily work quite like we think. Do you know

1 Quote attributed to Ted Johnson.

Jesus Christ as Savior and Lord of your life? No other affiliation or relationship can give you a right standing with God. And this relationship we have with Jesus is not a loose affiliation like we have with others where they do us favors, and we do favors for them. Our relationship with Jesus is based on the total commitment of our lives to Him and His kingdom.

In the last chapter, I talked about the religious lost who trust in their religious acts and rituals to get to heaven. By contrast, the affiliated lost count on their affiliations—not on God's grace and Christ's sacrifice—to get to heaven. They are members of a certain church or denomination. They have a relative who is a preacher. They have a spouse who follows Christ. They may even have a good relationship with the local church pastor. Regardless of the connection, though, they count on riding the coattails of church membership or some personal affiliation to get them to heaven. "But saving grace in Jesus Christ is not 'viral.' You can't catch it from someone else you are close to. It is the work of the Holy Spirit."[2] Here's why: Jesus says,

> *I am the way and the truth and the life.*
> *No one comes to the Father except through me.*
> John 14:6

This makes it clear that no affiliation other than a personal faith in Christ is going to make any of us right with God and get us to heaven.

---

2 Quote attributed to Louis Joseph.

Go Deeper

1. Do you know a lot of Christians?

2. Do you make decisions the way they do?

3. Do you know joy and peace?

4. Are you relying on your connections for favor with God?

"GOOD"

Most of us know a good, upstanding citizen in our community that does not claim any relationship with God. What does God say about that? Compared to His holiness and His requirements, they're not really good at all and still in need of a Savior.

As it is written:
"There is no one righteous, not even one;
there is no one who understands; there is no one who
seeks God."
Romans 3:10-11

Chapter 5

A number of people fit into this category. Raised with good moral and ethical values, they choose to live out those values and do so quite well. Compared to other people—both Christians and non-Christians—they are good people by societal standards. Many of these people don't go to church and don't want to because they live cleaner, better lives than many people they know who do go to church. They don't belong to any particular denomination and believe living a good life and doing the best they can is all that's required. I particularly hurt for these people because their arguments make perfectly good human sense, but they are spiritually way off the mark.

> *There is a way that appears to be right,*
> *but in the end it leads to death.*
> Proverbs 14:12

> *"Why do you ask me about what is good?" Jesus replied.*
> *"There is only One who is good. If you want to enter*
> *life, keep the commandments."*
> Matthew 19:17

I'm thinking of one individual in particular like this. I've watched this man for many years and know his morals and ethics are impeccable. I have said many times I would like to be able to live as good a life as he does. Yet, he doesn't claim to know Christ.

One time, I wrestled with this so much that I asked a pastor friend about it. I even wondered if maybe I wasn't saved. I claimed to have the Spirit of God living in me, but this gentleman, who did not make the same claim, led a better life than I.

My friend told me that the answer to this is easy: "You have an enemy of your soul who fights you at every turn to keep you from living out your faith. By contrast, Satan already has this other gentlemen deceived. Therefore, Satan makes it easy for him to live out his moral and ethical choices without the battle you face."

I saw the truth in what he was saying. I also thought how dangerous a state this is to live in. Scripture says that Satan is a liar, a deceiver, a destroyer, and a thief. So any time we rely on our own goodness rather than on God's grace and Christ's sacrifice, we are being deceived and face an eternity without God.

The "good person" doesn't have a consistent prayer life. He or she doesn't see the need for one. These people think that, because they are "good," if there is a God He will take care of what they need. In a jam, they may pray, expecting God to help, just because they have been so good.

Tom

I grew up in a small town with a man named Tom (name changed to protect his anonymity). Tom was a great guy. He was likable and kind, a good neighbor to those who lived around him and a great community citizen. He had a strong family life and was a good friend to those who knew him. He was outgoing, and nearly everyone liked him. Tom worked hard and tended (well) to his own business.

But Tom was adamant about one thing: he wanted nothing to do with church. This was clearly an exception to the rule in our community. Many folks tried to talk to Tom about his spiritual life, but he did not see the need for a relationship with God. In Tom's view, he was as good a man as the people going to church—and better than many. He loved to use his brother-in-law as an example of a churchgoing man who was not as good as he was. And he was right. The problem was, I doubt seriously if his brother-in-law was a true believer, either.

I don't want to create confusion here. In the broadest sense a person is either in the darkness or in the light. A person who is in the light—i.e., has been converted—can be in one of two conditions. He or she can be a maturing, Spirit-led Christian, or the person can be carnal. Some have come into the light but still have habits and behaviors from their pre-conversion days. This is why a lost person like Tom might look at these people and say, "I'm just as good as they are." The Toms don't understand that the person is still a baby Christian.

Jesus had some very harsh language for the Pharisees. He told them that they refused to enter the kingdom of God and were keeping others from entering.

> *Woe to you, teachers of the law and Pharisees,*
> *you hypocrites! You shut the door of the kingdom of*
> *heaven in people's faces. You yourselves do not enter,*
> *nor will you let those enter who are trying to.*
> *Woe to you, teachers of the law and Pharisees, you*
> *hypocrites! You travel over land and sea to win a*
> *single convert, and when you have succeeded,*
> *you make them twice as much a child of hell*
> *as you are.*
> Matthew 23:13-15

This is true of imitators who frequent the church. Also, it's sadly true of carnal believers who make the faith unattractive to those who haven't yet believed.

With guys like Tom, it's hard to make the case for a relationship with God. They make a few valid points based on relative goodness and badness of people that are hard to argue. The arguments can only be addressed from a spiritual and biblical standpoint. Poor souls like Tom are truly deceived because they don't understand what the Bible teaches about God's holiness, His wrath and righteousness, or how evil sin actually is. In their deception, they contend they are good, but the Bible says:

> *All of us have become like one who is unclean,*
> *and all our righteous acts are like filthy rags; we all shrivel*
> *up like a leaf, and like the wind our sins sweep us away.*
> Isaiah 64:6

> *We all, like sheep, have gone astray, each of us has*
> *turned to our own way; and the Lord has laid on him*

the iniquity of us all.
Isaiah 53:6

For all have sinned and fall short of the glory of God.
Romans 3:23

As it is written:
"There is no one righteous, not even one;
there is no one who understands;
there is no one who seeks God. All have turned away,
they have together become worthless;
there is no one who does good, not even one."
Romans 3:10-12

People who claim to be *good* have rejected what the holy Scriptures say about them. They define good on a relative basis by comparing themselves to others. This, of course, is nothing unusual. People tend to do that. In school, they compare themselves to little Johnny bad boy. Then they know that, relative to Johnny, they are good. People compare themselves to Hitler, Stalin, and other deeply evil men, and in doing so, they can feel good about themselves. The trouble is that God doesn't grade on a curve. His standard for judgment is the perfect life of His Son Jesus Christ. Anything short of that is an offense to a holy God and not acceptable.

Many would say that's unfair, but to think so simply means they don't understand the righteousness of God. God is completely righteous and holy in all His ways. But God is also loving and forgiving. That's why He gave His only Son to die on the cross to pay the penalty of our sins so that we could be made right with God. God takes sin seriously. Otherwise, why would He require the heavy payment He placed on Jesus, His Son?

Even people who presume that God grades on a curve have a problem. They have to figure out where God draws the line. Is it just north of Hitler? Just above a mass murderer or a hard-core thief? It's hard to know. People with this belief system can never really know for sure where they stand with God. That's why they often say they hope they are going to heaven. When time comes to meet their Maker, they tend to have a level of anxiety not experienced by a true believer because they're just not sure if they've been good enough. And the truth is *they haven't!*

A believer can be sure, though, because he or she placed all confidence in the perfect life of Jesus, and that is acceptable before God as payment for sins. Believers have no confidence in self. It's placed 100 percent in the sacrifice of Jesus Christ on the cross.

Scripture

Like anyone else, the "good" person can be saved only by accepting the authority of Scripture about what it takes to be saved. I base my beliefs on the teachings of the Bible. Why? Because it's been verified to be true. What do I mean by that?

There are over 400 prophecies in the Old Testament, and many of them were made hundreds of years before they played out in history. The statistical odds of even a few of those prophecies coming true are something like billions to one. And yet many have already played out, while others are in process. As a man with an accounting degree, I'm not comfortable betting against that kind of odds.

To draw a comparison: physical laws govern the universe, like gravity. It works 100 percent of the time. I don't understand it. I can't explain it in physics terms, but I know that it works all the time. The same is true of spiritual laws even though people sometimes refuse to see the obvious connections. With the law of gravity, there's an immediate cause-and-effect relationship which makes it easier to see that it works. With spiritual laws, though, there is often a lag between the cause and effect. Therefore people sometimes choose not to believe, but I have yet to see one of the spiritual laws discussed in Scripture that is not true.

The rich young ruler—someone in the New Testament who thought he was good based on his works—is an example of what I'm talking about. He asked Jesus what he must do to enter the kingdom of God. He really expected a commendation for all of his good works, especially when Jesus mentioned a few things such as loving God and loving his neighbor. The man said he had done those things ever since he was a child. Rather than argue with him, though, Jesus simply told him, "Go and sell all that you have and give to the poor." Jesus knew that the man really cared more about his possessions and power than he did about the kingdom of God. His perceived goodness would not get him into God's kingdom, and the man walked away sad.

Fortunately, there are also some scriptural examples of people who made the right choice. For instance, God sent the Apostle Peter to visit a man named Cornelius. He was a good man, known by his friends and neighbors as one who was righteous and generous to the poor. But he did not have the Spirit of Christ living in him. The difference between Cornelius and many others in this category is that he recognized that something was missing and had been praying for someone to come and show him exactly what was lacking in his life. Cornelius and his family gladly trusted in Jesus.

People who will not accept Scripture's truth have perhaps one other thing that could reach them: *the life of the Spirit-led Christian.* The upright moral life of "good" men or women goes only so far. They have a refined sense of fairness and what's right. They may even have elements of mercy to them. But a person who will be persecuted for his or her faith or a person who will consistently turn the other cheek, or that will go much further in demonstrating kindness, gentleness, and self-control than the "good" individual may cause them to pause and think about their beliefs.

This happened to the Apostle Paul. He observed the stoning of Stephen, a follower of Jesus, and approved it. Yet he was taken aback by Stephen's response to the people who stoned him. He asked God to forgive those who were killing him. Stephen died, not in fear or anger, but in great peace. I believe this was the start of the softening process for Paul before God appeared to him on the Damascus Road.

In the early church in Jerusalem, many were converted because of the way Christians lived. The hungry were fed. The sick were cared for. And those imprisoned were visited and comforted. The goodness of Christians went beyond the norms of society in that day. Others noticed the love and different life, and it led many to faith in Jesus Christ. *The same can still work today!* A story from World War II offers a fascinating example.

Mitsuo Fuchida was the leader of the Japanese attack on Pearl Harbor. He was eventually promoted during the war to be in charge of all Japanese air operations, and he considered himself an honorable citizen and a patriot. After the war, though, even he realized that wasn't enough, and his heart was changed. But what changed him? One part of the "softening process" was a speech by General MacArthur in which he said:

> The problem, basically, is spiritual and therefore requires a spiritual renewal and improvement of human character that will harmonize with our almost matchless advance in science, art, literature and with all the material and cultural developments of the past 2000 years. It must be of the spirit if we are to save the flesh. Let us pray that peace be now restored to the world and that God will preserve it always.[3]

Fuchida had expected a triumphant, arrogant speech from MacArthur. After all, the general could have bragged of America's power and victory, but he didn't—and Fuchida was impressed. When Christians think and act differently than the rest of the world, it catches the attention of non-believers and softens their hearts. MacArthur's speech was

3 T. Martin Bennett, *Wounded Tiger: A Nonfiction Novel* (Onstad Press, 2014).

the first impact on Fuchida's heart that eventually led to his conversion.

Later, the work of a young American girl named Peggy touched Fuchida. She worked among his people even though her father and mother were murdered by the Japanese. Peggy had gone back to Japan and ministered to the Japanese people in such a way that they could explain it only by the love of a God they did not know or understand. In his historical novel about Fuchida, T. Martin Bennett explains it this way:

> After his time with Kanegasaki a year earlier, he had interviewed others who were with him at the same relocation center to learn more about the girl who served them, Peggy. They all confirmed the same story. Fuchida was convinced she had a kind of genuine love that had stopped the cycle of revenge, but he couldn't understand where it came from. Certainly no one could love like this on his own. There had to be a secret.[4]

The secret, of course, was Jesus Christ at work in her life. And it's the same secret that will reach "good" people today.

---

4 Ibid., 419.

Go Deeper

1. Do you consider yourself a good person? If so, on what basis?

2. Are you willing to sacrifice significantly for the good of others?

3. Do you ever sin? What do you think the consequences will be?

THE REBELLIOUS AND HARDENED SOUL

Rebellious souls want nothing to do with God or His ways. They want their own way! The more they rebel against God, the harder and less sensitive their souls become. These are people who, after becoming aware of their sin and rebellion against God, continue on that path. They are selfish, want to be in charge of their own lives, and don't trust in God's plan for them. The danger for those who continue on this path is that the hardening soul eventually becomes a heart of stone.

Chapter 6

As time passes, the openly rebellious soul becomes a hardened soul. On my family farm when growing up, I worked hard with my hands. My hands started off soft and tender and sensitive to any kind of touch. As I continued to work, though, they developed callouses; they hardened. My calloused hands lost the sensitivity to touch that I once had. In fact, there were many things I couldn't feel at all anymore, and the same is true of a hardened heart. Things that once would have touched the soul, pierced it, made it feel sorrow, regret, remorse, and pain no longer have any impact on it. The hardened soul has no prayer life. There is no desire for communion and relationship with a holy God.

Why do I point this out? Because of how dangerous it is to continue in rebellion against our loving God.

We begin life with a conscience sensitive to the rebuke and direction of God's Spirit. The more times we push against it, though, the more layers of callouses build up. Hardening continues until we cannot sense, feel, or respond to God's direction in our lives. (This can also happen in a Christian's life, but only to a certain point). It is an extremely dangerous situation, like spiritual plaque building up in our souls. It's deadly—not just in this life but for eternity.

One of the two thieves crucified with Jesus is an example of a rebellious and hardened soul. We know this because even the actions of Jesus on the cross didn't change his heart. We also know this because the other thief was touched, recognized Jesus as the Messiah, and turned to Him in faith.

Many people believe that as long as we haven't drawn our last breath, it's not too late to turn to God, and in one sense, this may be true. I believe God always has a desire to seek and save those who are lost. The truth of Scripture, however, is that a person can rebel against God so many times and become so hard that he or she is no longer able respond to God's call.

> *This is the verdict: Light has come into the world,*
> *but people loved darkness instead of light because*
> *their deeds were evil.*
> John 3:19

> *And Pharaoh sent, and behold, not one of the livestock*
> *of Israel was dead. But the heart of Pharaoh was*
> *hardened, and he did not let the people go.*
> Exodus 9:7 (ESV)

> *But the LORD hardened the heart of Pharaoh, and*
> *he did not listen to them,*
> *as the LORD had spoken to Moses.*
> Exodus 9:12 (ESV)

This is a chilling word from God. Some people think God's judgment occurs when He corrects and chastises them to bring them into accord with His plan for their life. But the reality is that God's greatest judgment on this earth is when He no longer corrects and instead turns people over to their own selfish desires. He no longer pursues them, making it impossible for them to turn and come to salvation. We should remember that God says:

> *Because the Lord disciplines the one he loves,*
> *and he chastens everyone he accepts as his son.*
> Hebrews 12:6

But also:

> *Therefore God gave them over in the sinful desires of*
> *their hearts to sexual impurity for the degrading*
> *of their bodies with one another.*
> *They exchanged the truth about God for a lie,*
> *and worshiped and served created things*
> *rather than the Creator—*
> *who is forever praised. Amen.Because of this,*
> *God gave them over to shameful lusts. Even their*
> *women exchanged natural sexual relations*
> *for unnatural ones.*
> Romans 1:24-26

This is a very serious warning to those with the mindset that they can live any way they want to, then just before death seek God's mercy and come into His kingdom. While the Bible gives examples of people who did just that, it's not the norm, nor should it be counted on. Besides the risk of waiting until it's too late to turn to God, they waste opportunity while here on earth. After all, what do they think is the point of this life? These folks shun God all their lives and go their own way. Their "worst-case" attitude toward life after death is that they will just go to hell and party with their friends.

I believe and trust in God's mercy. I stake all of my eternal future on that and have absolutely no hope apart from God's mercy. Yet these people are deceived and, in a way, are counting on God's mercy even more than I do. They actually believe they can ignore God all their lives and want nothing to do with Him but also believe that He's going to provide a party room for them for all eternity. In reality, they are playing Russian roulette with their eternal souls. No one knows when Christ will return. Few people have any idea when their lives will be over. Even the most aggressive gambler would not bet against these odds. Why would anyone bet against them with his or her eternal soul?

The great irony is that these are often the same people who make fun of Christians. They consider us ignorant and living in "blind faith." Yet I have to ask the question: how much more blind faith can you have than that which they express? Scripture doesn't offer any hope or encouragement to these people. They're "making it up as they go along." It's true that Christ loves them and is patient to give them many chances before it is too late to turn to Him.

I have a caution here for Christians, too: it's not our job to decide that someone has reached the point of no return; it's God's. Most of us would have thought John Newton, the man who wrote the hymn "Amazing Grace," was beyond hope prior to his conversion. He was a hardened sailor, a slave ship captain, and a drunk, but if we thought he was past the point of no return, we would have been wrong. We should pray for and pursue the lost until God tells us in our spirit to stop.

World War II provides another example of how this works. An American soldier named Jake had a great effect on his enemies who were hardened sinners. Taken as a prisoner of war by the Japanese, he and his friends were treated terribly and often tortured by them. At one point, he vowed that he could never forgive his enemies, but God changed his heart. After finally coming home to the states, he had one overwhelming desire: to go back to Japan and minister to the people there. Here is what T. Martin Bennett said about him in his book, *Wounded Tiger*:

> He had no feelings of hatred toward his captors any longer. Waves of love seemed to have swept over him in the preceding days. He couldn't be angry if he wanted to be. Patting his face dry, his joy of being released was tempered by a sadness he felt for the Japanese people.[5]

Jake did return to Japan and ministered to many. He traveled and spoke to many about God's love. Yet at one point, he got discouraged, so his wife read him these words from a letter a young woman had sent him:

> I had always hated God, but through you, I was born as a child in the heavenly kingdom. Now the Lord is my light and my shield. I'm not afraid anymore.[6]

---

5 Bennett, 377.
6 Ibid., 423.

Even for the rebellious heart, there can be hope.

Go Deeper

1. Do you feel your soul getting harder year after year?

2. Do you really want to continue in this direction?

3. Do you know someone like this? If yes, are you praying for him or her? Is there anything this person can see in your life that would soften him or her?

Introduction to the Season of Light

The converted soul, sometimes referred to as reborn, has left the darkness to trust Jesus and follow Him. The direction of the changed life has shifted from self to Christ. The converted soul has a new perspective on life—like a captive that has been set free. Converted souls are free from the power and penalty of sin.

Chapter 7

The converted soul is one who has responded to the promptings of the Holy Spirit and accepted God's grace by trusting in Christ's sacrifice on the cross as full and complete payment for his or her sins. We would say this person has been born again. Converted souls have been born of the Spirit. They did nothing to earn their salvation but received it by God's grace through faith in Jesus Christ. They have trusted Jesus not only as Savior of their lives, but as Lord. They have made a decision to turn from self and from making all their decisions to serving Jesus as Lord of their lives with Him guiding their decisions. Converted souls do not do good works to earn salvation or to earn God's favor. Rather, they work out of love and gratitude for what God has done for them.

> *For we are God's handiwork, created in*
> *Christ Jesus to do good works,*
> *which God prepared in advance for us to do.*
> Ephesians 2:10

Fresh converts are fun to watch. They are excited about their newborn faith and want to tell others about it. They read Scripture and understand it in a way that was not possible before. They have a desire for the Word of God and things of God and to obey like never before.

Chuck Swindoll says that conversion happens in a moment but that sanctification takes a lifetime. How right he is. There are many stages of the faith walk—seasons of the soul—that people go through from the time of conversion until the time God takes them to heaven.

Seasons of the Converted Soul

In the following chapters, I identify 13 seasons in a converted soul's life. As I look back over my life from a spiritual perspective, I see that my soul has gone through several seasons. In fact, I repeated some of the seasons more than once, such as the Wilderness season and season of Solitude. As I study Scripture, I see the seasons of the soul that saints of the past went through and often recognize my story in theirs. I also see some seasons of theirs that I have not experienced yet, and I'm really excited about those. I look forward to the Sunset season, for instance, and growing in the season of Gratitude. I look forward to the Promised Land season and taking all that God has laid before me.

THE NEW LIFE

All new life starts at the infant stage, which needs to be especially nurtured and cared for. Otherwise, it won't survive. It's the same for a new Christian. It's an exciting time in the family of God, but this new Christian must be cared for.

Chapter 8

The day I became a Christian at age nine, I felt like an incredible burden had been lifted. I had a sense of peace and calm.

This stage of the spiritual walk is exciting because of the good things God wants to do for you and show you. The new and different quality of life is something the religious leaders in Jesus' day did not understand. For instance, when Nicodemus visited Jesus at night to find out how to enter God's kingdom, Jesus told him that he must be born again. Nicodemus thought he was talking about physical rather than spiritual birth and was confused.

When God created Adam and Eve in the Garden of Eden He gave them physical bodies and spirits that were alive and had daily communion with Him. When they chose to sin, they still had physical lives, but the spirit in them died, and they were separated from God. New birth occurs when that spirit is brought back to life. But how does this happen?

The spirit in Adam and Eve died because they walked away from God's goodness and His commandments. When we do a 180° turn and walk back toward God, asking forgiveness for our rebellion and sin and trusting in the sacrifice of Jesus on the cross for forgiveness of our sin, then our spirit comes to life. All things become new, and we see life differently because of the work of God. After their sin,

Adam and Eve needed to look to Christ for forgiveness, just as we do.

Growing in Faith

As we grow in faith, God does incredible things to build our faith, just as a parent does "incredible" things helping children to learn and grow. I saw this with my younger children many times, but even as they grew, the process continued. During their college years, for example, they periodically called home, worried about a test and afraid they wouldn't do well. When I asked if they had studied and done the best they could, they would assure me they had. Listening to their concerns, I sometimes guessed they might be heading toward a C for a final on which they needed a B. They were asking me to pray with them for a B, so again, I would ask if they had done their best. With their assurance of the appropriate hard work done, I would often say we're going to the God of the universe and would remind my concerned student that God can easily make it possible to get an A. I wanted to pray for an A because something more important than the grade was at stake. I knew they were at the stage of spiritual growth in which God was building their faith by answering legitimate prayers. The exciting outcome is the remarkable number of times the kids got grades above what they thought was possible simply because we went to God in prayer.

I knew it was a special time and that God would do incredible things to build my children's faith. Seeing God in an obvious way would then encourage them to come to Him again and again in prayer. Along the way, though, I pointed out that there would come a day when they were more mature, and even though they might ask, God would not answer their prayers in the way they thought He should or even the way He had in the past. I wanted them to understand that as you mature in the faith, challenges get harder. As we grow, God doesn't respond as quickly or in the ways we think He should—not because He doesn't love us, but because He's taking us deeper.

> *Therefore, since we have been justified by faith,*
> *we have peace with God*
> *through our Lord Jesus Christ. Through him we have*
> *also obtained access by faith*
> *into this grace in which we stand, and we rejoice in*
> *hope of the glory of God.*
> *More than that, we rejoice in our sufferings,*
> *knowing that suffering produces endurance,*
> *and endurance produces character,*
> *and character produces hope,*
> *and hope does not put us to shame,*
> *because God's love has been poured into our hearts*
> *through the Holy Spirit who has been given to us.*
> Romans 5:1-5 (ESV)

The Struggle

When we are converted, our desires shift, and our understanding of Scripture changes, but we have lifelong habits and thought patterns that aren't transformed overnight. The Apostle Paul recognized this and referred to the Corinthian

Christians as babies in Christ. He acknowledged that they had been converted but was concerned for their spiritual growth. They were not thinking or acting any differently than the pagans around them. Paul desired that they go deeper and grow in their faith:

> *Brothers and sisters, I could not address you as*
> *people who live by the Spirit but as people who are still*
> *worldly—mere infants in Christ.*
> *I gave you milk, not solid food,*
> *for you were not yet ready for it.*
> *Indeed, you are still not ready.*
> *You are still worldly. For since there is jealousy and*
> *quarreling among you, are you not worldly?*
> *Are you not acting like mere humans?*
> 1 Corinthians 3:1-3

One thing we do have as new converts is the power of choice. We can choose to do things God's way or our way. Scripture says that the mind set on the flesh is death, but the mind set on the Spirit is life:

> *Those who live according to the flesh have their minds*
> *set on what the flesh desires;*
> *but those who live in accordance with the Spirit have*
> *their minds set on what the Spirit desires.*
> *The mind governed by the flesh is death, but the mind*
> *governed by the Spirit is life and peace.*
> *The mind governed by the flesh is hostile to God;*
> *it does not submit to God's law, nor can it do so.*
> *Those who are in the realm of the flesh cannot please God.*
> Romans 8:5-8

Paul is referring to spiritual death and life, but his words also have a practical application. When we do things according to God's Spirit, we discover a life of opportunity, of relationships, and of goodness and holiness. By contrast, when we work against God's guidance, we experience the death of all those things.

One way to know whether or not you're being guided by the Spirit is to consider if you are making decisions that run contrary to your normal thinking and reactions. In other words, if you're normally not a patient person, but are you exercising patience in a particular situation, you're probably following the Spirit. If you're typically not a bold person, but you are inspired to take a stand that is uncomfortable for you, you're probably doing it by the Spirit of God.

Confusion

Discerning your own connection with the Spirit can be confusing because Satan quickly tries to steal away the joy, faith, and confidence you have. It can also be confusing because you may want to walk in the Spirit but find yourself repeatedly failing by walking in the flesh.

While this conflict works against every believer, there's a particular struggle for new converts. They have a newfound excitement about things of the Lord, but Satan begins to cause them to doubt. They struggle with obedience, so Satan tells them the conversion wasn't real, and he steals their faith. This can be a very trying time and, unfortunately for some people, can last for years. It did for me. I struggled with confidence in my conversion experience for a long time even though I desperately wanted to walk consistently in the strength of God's Spirit. In Romans 7, Paul describes his own battle with this:

> We know that the law is spiritual; but I am unspiritual, sold as a slave to sin. I do not understand what I do. For what I want to do I do not do, but what I hate I do. And if I do what I do not want to do, I agree that thelaw is good. As it is, it is no longer I myself who do it, but it is sin living in me.
> Romans 7:14-17

> For in my inner being I delight in God's law; but I see another law at work in me, waging war against the law of my mind and making me a prisoner of the law of sin at work within me. What a wretched man I am! Who will rescue me from this body that is subject to death? Thanks be to God, who delivers me through Jesus Christ our Lord!
> Romans 7:22-25

Notice that he calls himself "a wretched man" because he can't seem to do the things he really wants to do. He poses the question: who will save me? And his answer is Jesus Christ. We often admire Paul's faith, but forget that he had to struggle, too.

What If You Die as an Immature (Baby) Christian?

It's hard to think of anything more tragic than the death of a baby. Parents mourn, family mourns, friends mourn, and even people that didn't know the child mourn. It is the most heartbreaking of all human losses.

In our spiritual lives, it is similarly heartbreaking for a Christian to die as a baby. All of us were created and saved in order to grow in our spiritual lives. Yet some people die in the baby stage. Scripture even speaks to this when it says that sometimes God takes people home early because they are failing to develop in their Christian walk. While God may let them die as baby Christians, He never intended it to be this way. He wants us to grow strong in the faith and to experience joy and peace.

Summary

What is New Life like?

It's exciting but can also be confusing and a struggle. Your *prayer* life will tend to be simple, innocent, and focused more on helping with your own needs and struggles rather than intercession for others and Kingdom causes.

What is God's purpose?

To grow us up in the faith. To make us strong.

What is the proper response?

Continue in prayer, Bible study, and fellowship with believers individually and in small groups. Continue to trust God in all matters.

Go Deeper

1. Have you trusted Christ as your Lord and Savior?

2. Have you experienced a newfound peace and joy?

3. Has Satan caused you to have doubts about your experience?

4. How are you growing in your faith?

*F*AITH-*B*UILDING

As soon as we enter the Kingdom of God through faith in Christ, Satan starts trying to tear us down, and God works to build us up. The things God does to build our faith are incredible.

Chapter 9

The Faith-Building season is like spring, full of life and new growth. King David experienced a season of faith building before he entered his wilderness experience. As a young boy tending sheep, God was with him and even helped David kill a lion and a bear:

> *But David said to Saul, "Your servant has been keeping his father's sheep. When a lion or a bear came and carried off a sheep from the flock, I went after it, struck it and rescued the sheep from its mouth. When it turned on me, I seized it by its hair, struck it and killed it. Your servant has killed both the lion and the bear; this uncircumcised Philistine will be like one of them, because he has defied the armies of the living God. The Lord who rescued me from the paw of the lion and the paw of the bear will rescue me from the hand of this Philistine." Saul said to David, "Go, and the Lord be with you."*
> 1 Samuel 17:34-37

His experiences as a shepherd built David's faith so that when the time came to fight Goliath, he had the courage. Overcoming the giant in battle built his faith even further, so David would be ready for other fights in which God would give him victory.

When you get serious about your walk with God, He gets serious about building your faith.

Consider it pure joy, my brothers and sisters, whenever you face trials of many kinds, because you know that the testing of your faith produces perseverance.
James 1:2-3

I had a couple of these life-changing experiences in my thirties. As the Assistant Vice President of Internal Audit for Hospital Corporation of America, I was frustrated and felt stuck. It looked like several years would pass before my boss retired, and I didn't really have anywhere else to go in the department or the company—at least it felt like I didn't. And to make matters worse, my boss wasn't a particularly good "PR" man. He frequently said things that caused the company leadership to think less of him and our department. So my main supporter was not respected and neither was the functional area I worked in!

Then I got a call from another healthcare company. It was considerably smaller than HCA, but the company offered me the title of Senior Vice President of Internal Audit, along with a 20 percent raise and what seemed like a large amount of stock options. The package included a company-paid country club membership and a company car, the equivalent of a large Cadillac at that time. Every friend and confidant I talked to said it was an "offer I couldn't refuse" and that they would miss me. Yet, I didn't have peace about it.

I was deeply involved in teaching young single adults at my church, and my wife and I lived only about two-and-ahalf hours away from each of our parents. My new job location would add another six hours to any trip home. Not only that, my kids were settled and happy, and my wife enjoyed her work in Nashville. When I really prayed about it and asked who was benefiting from this move, the answer kept coming back that I was the primary beneficiary. A change would require sacrifice or loss for family, church, and friends, and I just didn't sense it was what God wanted me to do. I finally turned the offer down, thinking in my heart that my ship would never come again, or if it did, it would be several more years.

Within nine months of that time, though, significant changes happened. First, the company that had offered me the job went bankrupt, and the senior officers—of whom I would have been one—were sued. Second, my boss at HCA retired earlier than expected, and I was promoted to a job I thought I would have to wait several more years for. Third, I got a good raise, a company car, and about seven times the value of the equity I would have gotten from the other company—even if it had been successful! That taught me a great lesson about walking by faith rather than by sight. This all occurred when I was 30 and 31—early enough to serve me well many times in the future.

Round Two

I grew in that position, and everything went well—beyond my talent or ability. Then *it happened*. The company I worked for—which had acquired many other organizations—was itself acquired. The acquisition merged three once-separate companies and three different cultures. Yet when I learned more about the situation, I was not worried because I thought I was surely the best qualified in the organization to lead the Internal Audit Department.

God also gave me favor and grace with the new leadership of the company. In fact, they wanted me to take a corporate operations role within the company, saying they thought my talent was not fully utilized in Internal Audit. However, after much prayer, I knew God was leading me to stay in Internal Audit. I explained this to company leadership, and they said okay. In the process, though, a miscommunication cropped up through which the lead auditor in the acquiring company had been offered the job as Vice President of Internal Audit.

This result left me, a vice president, reporting to another vice president—in many ways, a humbling, awkward, and uncomfortable relationship. To further complicate my situation, the new corporate headquarters was in Louisville instead of Nashville, and I found myself on a chartered plane most weeks, flying to Louisville for a day or two of meetings with my new boss. I wondered how this could be happening and remember going to church one Sunday morning and pleading with God for answers. He gave me a clear answer through that morning's Scripture reading:

> *Listen, King Jehoshaphat and all who live in Judah*
> *and Jerusalem! This is what the Lord says to you:*
> *"Do not be afraid or discouraged because of this vast army.*
> *For the battle is not yours, but God's."*
> 2 Chronicles 20:15

I'll never forget those words: the battle is mine not yours, says the Lord. Then I watched as God worked on my behalf to turn around a bad situation.

Although I had dreaded having a new boss, it turned out to be one of the more pleasant surprises of God's grace. My boss and I talked openly and honestly. I even explained that my decision to remain in Internal Audit was based on God's leading, despite the other offers from company leadership. I did not know his spiritual faith walk at the time, but his response resonated. He said, "God works in strange and mysterious ways." And He certainly did. I enjoyed the next year far more than I thought I would.

Within about a year, the company announced that corporate headquarters would relocate to Nashville, and since my boss chose not to move, he recommended me as the best person to take over his job. By that time, though, the company had acquired another large healthcare organization, and the leader of that other organization, who became the new chairman of the board, decided to promote his internal auditor to be the lead auditor. The man was a personal friend of mine, and the thought of him taking the job that I thought would be mine made the situation awkward and uncomfortable. Then one day in an executive meeting, the new organization chart was handed out. Not only had I been tapped as the lead auditor, but I had been promoted to Senior Vice President of Audit!

That situation led to a season in which God's grace and favor just seemed to follow me. Everything I did was viewed favorably by those around me, and anything negative seemed to get attributed to someone else. It built my faith to a whole new level.

After what I'd been through, I thought I could face and endure anything, but little did I know my next test would be even harder. As I had just done, I wanted again to watch as God fought the next battle, but that wasn't His plan. I was about to be tested to the limits of my being. I'll explain more later, but first let me tell you more about Jake.

As a prisoner of war, held by the Japanese, during World War II, Jake struggled with his faith. Here was his condition at one point:

The boils under his skin had come back over his entire body. Each one ached with continuous pain, yet there was no relief in the darkness. After collapsing several times and blacking out, he was finally permitted to lie on a filthy straw mat. Jake sensed his body beginning to shut down. He drifted in and out of reality. The screaming, the darkness, the pain, all combined to bring him to the edge of delirium. As much as he may have wanted to, he had little strength to even scream. During this terrible time, something inside him told him to ask for help. He remembered the scriptures he had studied that if he had the faith of just a tiny mustard seed that mountains could be moved. He took a chance and asked God for healing and he really believed God would answer. He decided he would just keep praying until he got an answer—or simply passed out and collapsed onto the floor. Next he thought he heard a voice telling him he was free. Within a few days, he was treated by doctors and eating soup, bread, boiled eggs, and fresh milk.[7]

And here's what God did to strengthen Jake's "mustard seed" faith:

> That night, as Jake lay on his back in the darkness, in the stench surrounded by the echoes of cries of unknown men, he smiled as he took a bite of bread. "You keep your promises, God," he said with tear-filled eyes. [8]

God knows when He needs to work on your behalf to build your faith. Trust Him with that season.

---

7 Bennett, 346.
8 Ibid., 347.

Summary

Why does the Faith-Building season occur?
To increase our faith.

What is the result?
More confidence in God and less confidence in self.

What should we do?
Pray in faith, in accordance with God's will, and then watch how He answers our prayers. The prayer life in this season will tend to be simple and will tend to focus on asking for provision and help in troubles.

Go Deeper

1. Are you growing in your faith? Describe how.

2. What do you trust God for right now?

3. What are you struggling with right now that you haven't turned over to God?

PRIDE

....

Pride is a deceitful and subtle thing. God sent the children of Israel into the wilderness to humble them and to test them. Why do slaves need to be humbled? We think of proud people as those who are rich and arrogant. I grew up very poor. Yet poor people can be proud. Slaves can be proud. Anyone can be proud. But beware, because "pride precedes a fall"!

Be careful that you do not forget the Lord your God, failing to observe his commands, his laws and his decrees that I am giving you this day. Otherwise, when you eat and are satisfied, when you build fine houses and settle down, and when your herds and flocks grow large and your silver and gold increase and all you have is multiplied, then your heart will become proud and you will forget the Lord your God, who brought you out of Egypt, out of the land of slavery.
Deuteronomy 8:11-14

Chapter 10

Pride goes before destruction,
a haughty spirit before a fall.
Proverbs 16:18

For everything in the world—
the lust of the flesh, the lust of the eyes,
and the pride of life—comes not from
the Father but from the world.
The world and its desires pass away,
but whoever does the will of God lives forever.
1 John 2:16-17

Proverbs wisely says that pride precedes a fall. It goes on to say that whoever humbles himself God will lift up and whoever exalts himself God will humble. Pride was the source of the fall of Satan when he said, "I will be like the Most High." And if we are not careful, it will be our downfall as well.

Pride tends to follow a season where we have experienced God's blessings. God warned the children of Israel after He blessed them by leading them into the Promised Land to be careful lest they would think their prosperity had come from their own intelligence and hard work. This is a great warning for us, too.

King David fell into this pride trap. God had blessed him

in every way possible. Yet what did David do? Instead of being humble and grateful, he got lazy and proud. He had been so successful in building a great army that he no longer felt it necessary to go do the hard work of leading them into battle. So one time, he sent them out while he stayed at home, lounging in the palace.

During this "sabbatical" from war, he saw a woman that he wanted: Bathsheba. Because he was king, he decided he would just take her—even though she was already married to one of his soldiers. Bathsheba became pregnant from her affair with David, so to fix the problem, the king tried to use his power to deceive her husband into thinking the baby was the husband's legitimate child. And when that didn't work, he used his power to have the husband killed.

David's pride led to one sin after another. So is God's Word true? Does pride lead to a fall? Yes! Though God was merciful to David and did not take his life, He told the king that the sword would never depart from his family—and it didn't.

One difference of this season from the other seasons is that both believers and unbelievers can be tripped up by pride. For example, King Nebuchadnezzar, a non-believer, was filled up with pride after God blessed him. Scripture reports Nebuchadnezzar's evaluation of his own standing—and God's response:

> He said, "Is not this the great Babylon I have built as
> the royal residence, by my mighty power and for the
> glory of my majesty?" Even as the words were
> on his lips, a voice came from heaven,

"This is what is decreed for you, King Nebuchadnezzar:
Your royal authority has been taken from you. You
will be driven away from people and will live with the
wild animals; you will eat grass like the ox.
Seven times will pass by for you until you acknowledge
that the Most High is sovereign over all kingdoms on
earth and gives them to anyone he wishes."
Immediately what had been said about Nebuchadnezzar
was fulfilled. He was driven away from people and ate
grass like the ox. His body was drenched with the dew
of heaven until his hair grew like the feathers of an
eagle and his nails like the claws of a bird.

Daniel 4:30-33

What happened to Nebuchadnezzar? He was like a wild animal of the field eating grass until he humbled himself and acknowledged the sovereignty of God.

You don't have to be to the ruler of a mighty empire to be tripped up by pride, though. More than once in my roles at HCA I (sadly!) tripped over God's warning myself. I say tripped instead of forgot because there were times when I was mindful of the need to stay humble and even thought I was. But I was not.

When HCA was acquired by a smaller company, I naturally assumed I was the most qualified to lead the Audit Department and made the assumption that would just happen, but instead, as I explained in the last chapter, I found myself as a vice president reporting to a vice president in another city for a year. That had a much-needed humbling effect on me.

Then, after humbling me, God blessed me again for several years. But guess what. I got proud again. Can you believe it? God had prospered my career, and I had multiple corporate functions under my oversight. Then, a series of events changed my world almost overnight. Instead of having several corporate functions under my supervision and approximately 300 employees, I had no functions at all under my authority.

When God says pride precedes a fall, He means it. Pride is very deceitful. We all must be careful lest we fall! The Bible calls it chastisement or being rebuked, and we'll talk more about that in the next chapter.

> *My son, do not despise the Lord's discipline,*
> *and do not resent his rebuke,*
> *because the Lord disciplines those he loves,*
> *as a father the son he delights in.*
> Proverbs 3:11-12

Summary
....

Why does the season of Pride occur?

One of the main reasons is that we start to take credit for God's blessings in our lives.

What is the result?

Chastisement or punishment aimed at correcting the sin and humbling us.

What should we do?

Stop the sin! Humble ourselves quickly so that God's chastening can end. One evidence of humbling ourselves is a vibrant prayer life. The proud person doesn't have a good prayer life because he or she does not feel dependent on God. The humble person knows that dependence on God is necessary for everything.

Go Deeper

1. Are you a proud person?

2. Do you think you are better or smarter than certain people?

3. Can you hold your head high before God?

4. Are you afraid others will find out what you are really like?

5. If you have found any pride in your life, what have you done with it?

CHASTISEMENT

Whoever spares the rod hates their children,
but the one who loves their children is careful to
discipline them.
Proverbs 13:24

Because the Lord disciplines the one he loves,
and he chastens everyone he accepts as his son.
Endure hardship as discipline; God is treating you as
his children.
For what children are not disciplined by their father?
Hebrew 12:6-7

We think of discipline in negative terms. We see it only as a result of anger, but Scripture teaches that God disciplines His children out of love.

Punishment is intended to hurt. Discipline is intended to correct and produce holiness.

God disciplines us because He loves us. He disciplines pride and other sins. His purpose is to put us on the right path to receive His best. And once the sin stops, the discipline stops.

They [our parents] disciplined us for a little while
as they thought best;
but God disciplines us for our good, in order that we
may share in his holiness.
Hebrews 12:10

Chapter 11

M any people see God as a grumpy, stern disciplinarian. But even though God's discipline can be severe, His attitude toward us is very different than what we imagine. Let's look at some scriptures that demonstrate God's approach:

> *That he might humble you and test you,*
> *to do you good in the end.*
> Deuteronomy 8:16 (ESV)

> *Whoever spares the rod hates their children,*
> *but the one who loves their children is careful to*
> *discipline them.*
> Proverbs 13:24

> *Because the Lord disciplines the one he loves,*
> *and he chastens everyone he accepts as his son.*
> *Endure hardship as discipline;*
> *God is treating you as his children.*
> *For what children are not disciplined by their father?*
> Hebrews 12:-6-7

> *Nevertheless, when we are judged in this way*
> *by the Lord, we are being disciplined so that we will*
> *not be finally condemned with the world.*
> 1 Corinthians 11:32

What is the constant that we see in these scriptures? God's love! God disciplines us because He loves us. His disciplines are severe because He loves us so much. He has such great plans and such a bright future for us that He is willing to see us suffer significantly rather than miss His best for us. King David realized this when he said:

> *Before I was afflicted I went astray,*
> *but now I obey your word.*
> Psalm 119:67

He realized that God's discipline saved him from some really bad things, and he was grateful. But Scripture has some words of warning to those who resist discipline:

> *My son, do not despise the Lord's discipline,*
> *and do not resent his rebuke,*
> *because the Lord disciplines those he loves,*
> *as a father the son he delights in.*
> Proverbs 3:11-12

As a young man, I struggled significantly at one point in my Christian walk. Looking back, I see clearly it was because of my double-mindedness and backsliding. My dad once wisely asked me if I had ever been aware of God's chastening or discipline in my life. It seemed like a strange question at the time, but over the years I learned the importance of it. Apparently, it was an important part of my dad's walk with the Lord. He told me about a time in his early years on the farm when he strayed from God. He had no interest in God or fellowship with other believers and was totally absorbed in trying to make a living on his farm. At the time, he had a bunch of sheep, but many of them got sick and died. He was even taking care of some sheep owned by my uncle, and they died, too! When my dad finally started walking with the Lord again, the animals stopped dying. As I think back about my childhood and Daddy's leadership of the family, I understand now why we were at church three times a week and every night during the fall revival.

Be aware, though, that it's easy to misunderstand this kind of lesson, become a legalist, and as a result have no more impact on the Kingdom than a pre-converted legalist. Legalists focus more on rules and rituals and less on relationship with the living God. You can be an unconverted legalist like the Pharisees. You can also be a converted legalist like the Galatians. Though the Galatians had been genuinely converted, they were returning to a focus on rituals and rules. I struggle with some of the same tendencies myself, but the more I—or any of us—determine to make relationship with God primary, the less legalism will appeal. And we can shorten the season of chastisement that comes with pride.

Summary

What is Chastisement like?
It feels like you are being beaten.

What is the purpose of the season?
Discipline, so that you return to God.

What is the proper response?
Stop sinning. Soon after the sin stops, the discipline can stop. Pray that God will reveal any unconfessed sin in your life. Listen to the slightest touch of the Holy Spirit. Respond quickly and completely as God leads you.

Go Deeper

1. Do you feel you are out of step with God? If so, how?

2. Do you sense God may be disciplining you because of unrepented sin in your life? If so, what will you do?

THE *P*RUNING *S*EASON

You don't get the best plants by just letting them grow. Grape vines, for example, grow more grapes if you prune them. Since grape plants default to growing new foliage rather than more grapes, you prune grape plants to produce more grapes. You cut out new foliage. Similarly, when you produce spiritual fruit, God will prune you. He will cut out some activities to put the focus on what will produce even more Kingdom fruit.

Chapter 12

G rowing up on a farm, I gained an understanding of how the pruning process works and why it is needed. And even though I live in the city now, I am fortunate enough to have six acres of land. I love nature. I love trees. I love pretty shrubs. And fortunately, in learning how to care for them, I'm well acquainted with how pruning works.

Three years ago, I grew a number of rose bushes. They reached shoulder high alongside my koi pond, but that winter, in February, I cut them back to about two feet tall. The casual observer would ask why anyone would take shoulder-high bushes and cut them back so much. Yet the reason is simple. Pruning makes the bushes healthier and prettier. By the end of summer, my roses were more gorgeous than ever before. You see, as bushes grow, they get long and lanky. Although "long and lanky" rose bushes still produce pretty roses, they don't have nearly as many blooms as a pruned rose bush. A pruned bush also has a healthier and stronger base for its foliage.

On a trip to the Napa Valley in California one time, I was impressed by the incredible vineyards there. I couldn't help but notice how perfectly trimmed and groomed the grapevines were. Grapes tend to grow vigorously, and a lot of wood must be cut away each year. Otherwise, the vines can become so dense that the sun cannot reach into the area where the fruit should form. Left to itself, a grapevine will always favor new growth over more grapes.

So how does this relate to the pruning season in a Christian's life? Bruce Wilkinson says it well in his book, *Secrets of the Vine*:

> If your life bears some fruit, God will intervene to prune you. His purpose is for you to cut away any immature commitments and lessen your priorities to make room for even greater abundance for his glory.[9]

We live in a culture that believes more is better, but in doing so, we reject some clear teachings of the Bible—like pruning, through which less is actually more.

A lawyer once asked Jesus to summarize the teachings of the Law. Jesus replied, "Love God with all your heart and your neighbor as yourself." In Matthew, Jesus teaches:

> *But seek first his kingdom and his righteousness,*
> *and all these things will be given to you as well.*
> Matthew 6:33

Jesus teaches the clear truth that, by narrowing our priorities, we can be more and accomplish more. A clear teaching of Scripture, for example, is the necessity of the Sabbath day and other periods of rest. Why did God emphasize that so much? Because He made us and knew what would be best for us over the long run. God knew that if we take periods to rest, we will actually accomplish

9 Bruce Wilkinson, *Secrets of the Vine* (Sisters, OR: Multnomah, 2001), 58.

more than we would by working seven days a week. This has been proven in many ways and was even the subject of a movie. In this story of dog racing, one man rested his dogs in regular cycles. The other people in the race just kept pushing their dogs with no rest, but the man who rested his dogs won the race.

Generally, "Type A" business leaders struggle with this. They think they can get ahead by just continuing to keep pressing rather than having seasons of rest and good vacations. But I know from experience that without the downtime, your creativity is reduced, your problem-solving ability loses its edge, your emotions get frayed, and you're not as effective in your interpersonal relationships. Your spiritual life gets short-circuited, and you spend less time in the Word and in prayer. As a result, you end up making decisions in the flesh versus the spirit, and this will always result in your making mistakes that have to be remedied.

Often, trials, discipline, and pruning all feel pretty much the same. They hurt! "Trials are intended to produce faith, discipline to produce holiness, and pruning to produce Kingdom fruit."[10]

> *I am the true vine, and my Father is the gardener.*
> *He cuts off every branch in me that bears no fruit,*
> *while every branch that does bear fruit he prunes so*
> *that it will be even more fruitful.*
> John 15:1-2

---

10 Quote attributed to Dick Wells.

Elijah

The Old Testament prophet Elijah went through a significant pruning season. God stripped all his daily routines and activities from him, then hid him in the wilderness in complete solitude. A stream provided water for Elijah, and he was fed daily by ravens that brought him food. He lived like this for three years!

What was God doing? He was preparing Elijah to oppose the 400 prophets of Baal and lead God's people back to God. Elijah would ultimately pray in front of all the people for fire to come down from heaven to burn his sacrifice and the water in the trenches to humiliate the other prophets. He would also pray publicly for rain after a three-year drought—and it would begin to rain. It took significant spiritual preparation for him to be ready to do all this.

Personal

One of my own pruning seasons came after a period of intense activity. I had worked hard and thought I was accomplishing a lot. I believed I was good at managing priorities and being very productive. Then I found out I had colon cancer.

The illness required me to take time off, which I discovered was much needed for rest and reflection. After a while, I phased back into my work routine, first for two hours a day, then four, then six, and finally to a full schedule, but what I learned during this time was invaluable.

Working two and four hours a day, I had to be very focused

on my priorities. I really had to think about what mattered most in order to produce a result. I had to think hard about what I needed to spend time on versus what somebody else could do.

My priorities became so clear that it gave greater clarity to the rest of my team. I did not spend any time looking into matters that they were perfectly capable of handling. I would only waste their valuable time by doing that. The end result was that my whole team got more done as I spent significantly less time at the office.

What was the purpose of this pruning? God knew what was coming. He knew my next assignment and knew that I would need to be clear about priorities. I would have to change my leadership style to handle the challenges He would give me next. To my surprise, God intended to leave me at HCA as President of Physician Services, but He also led me to the executive pastor role at our church for three years, part-time.

When my pastor first suggested I consider the position, I laughed but offered the obligatory "I'll pray about it." Nothing in me thought I was supposed to quit my job and join the staff at church. But as I prayed, it became clear that I was supposed to do something. God eventually led me to talk to the leadership of my company to be given flexibility so I could take on the executive pastor role at my church. The goals and my job at HCA were not reduced, but the needs of the church were growing. My prior season of pruning, however, helped me refocus on what was important, and it allowed me the margin to achieve my goals at HCA while helping my church with a major building and growth phase for three years.

I experienced firsthand that God does prune and cut out meaningless activities in your life by whatever means He has to so as to prepare you for a season of greater growth for His kingdom. Sounds great, right? So what's the problem? Simply this: unless you understand God's ways of developing your soul, you can confuse the season of pruning with a season of chastisement. When you're being pruned, if you act like you're being disciplined and fight against it, you can actually miss God's best and cause a season of discipline that you could have avoided.

So how do you know if you are being pruned versus disciplined? The pain they bring feels about the same. If you are being disciplined, there is sin in your life the Holy Spirit is trying to convict you of. But if you are being pruned, God is trying to cut some activities out of your life so you can be more focused on Kingdom work.

> The purpose of discipline is repentance and course correction. The purpose of pruning is to cut out the lesser priorities in your life to create room for greater Kingdom growth. It's important that you never confuse the two.[11]

The person being pruned likely has a very busy life, and this tends to result in less time spent in prayer. Our prayer lives, though, reveal priorities and direction from

---

11 Wilkinson.

God. Pruning is much easier if we have a vibrant prayer life so we focus more readily on those things God wants us engaged in.

Summary

What is Pruning like?

It hurts. It feels unfair. It looks and feels like Chastisement.

What is God's purpose?

Clearing out lesser priorities to make room for greater Kingdom growth.

What is the proper response?

Cooperate with God and focus on His priorities for your life.

Go Deeper

1. Is God removing things you cherish from your life? What are they?

2. Do you have any recurring, unconfessed sin in your life? If so, what is it?

3. Is God focusing you more on His priorities?

THE WILDERNESS SEASON

Before Jesus started His earthly ministry, He went to the desert to be tested.

When God called Abraham to leave his home and become the father of a great nation, He led him to the desert where He tested him.

Before God led the children of Israel to the Promised Land, He led them to the desert to test them.

When God is preparing you for a time of greater significance and influence, you, too, will go through the "wilderness experience."

Chapter 13

When God is preparing His people for an expanded ministry or getting them ready for a new, broader phase of life, Scripture shows that His pattern is to take people through a wilderness experience. In fact, in my study of Scripture, I have not seen any significant biblical figure that God did not lead through such an experience.

Jesus

God led Christ into the wilderness before He began His earthly ministry. There Jesus prayed and fasted for 40 days and was tested. These are tests recorded in the New Testament:

The tempter came to him and said,
"If you are the Son of God, tell these stones to become
bread." Then the devil took him to the holy city and
had him stand on the highest point of the temple.
"If you are the Son of God," he said,
"throw yourself down. For it is written:
"He will command his angels concerning you,
and they will lift you up in their hands,
so that you will not strike your foot against a stone."
Jesus answered him, "It is also written:
'Do not put the Lord your God to the test.'"
Again, the devil took him to a very high mountain

and showed him all the kingdoms of the world and
their splendor. "All this I will give you," he said,
"if you will bow down and worship me."
Matthew 4:3, 5-8

In these tests, the devil questioned the Word of God just as he had done with Eve in the Garden of Eden. In Genesis 3:1, Satan asked, "Did God say?" to sow doubt in Eve's mind. Satan tests Jesus by challenging Him to misuse His God-given gifts—for worldly success and prosperity—if He will worship Satan instead of God the Father. Satan uses the same temptations on us today.

The purpose of these tests were so Jesus would be clear about His ministry and fully grasp that fame, fortune, greatness, and abuse of God's care and provision were not something He would pursue. I believe in one phase of life or another, we all must make the same decisions as we choose to follow God's plan for our lives.

David

David was anointed king as a young man and served faithfully in Saul's kingdom. It was a great surprise to him, however, that he would go through a wilderness season before he would actually become king. He found himself hiding out and always on the run from the madman, Saul, who was king at the time. Often, David prayed to God and asked, "How long?" And it turned out his wilderness season lasted 12 years!

Israelites

Let's look at the children of Israel to understand the wilderness experience more fully. The book of Exodus tells of how God led His people out of slavery in Egypt into the desert. This was to prepare them for the Promised Land. Many years before, God had promised to the children of Israel the land of Canaan, a land flowing with milk and honey. Yet they did not go straight to the Promised Land from Egypt because of fear in their life.

Traveling a direct route into the Promised Land would have taken only a few days. Instead, Israel wandered in circles for 40 years in the wilderness while God prepared a nation of people suitable to enter the Promised Land. He wanted them to have a heart to achieve His plan.

Abraham

I guess it is just human nature that every time God makes a grand promise to us that we think we go directly to that position or state of being without going through the wilderness experience. But it was not true for the children of Israel. It was not even true for the father of the faith, Abraham. Remember, God told him to leave his home and go to a place that He would show him. Abraham naturally expected God's blessings on him for his obedience, but where did Abraham find himself? In the wilderness, of course.

Abraham unwisely took matters into his own hands and fled to Egypt and suffered the consequences of his decisions there. When God was through, He sent Abraham back to the wilderness, and that's a lesson for all of us.

When God sends us to a wilderness, we need to stay there until we learn all that God wants to teach us. If we take matters into our own hands, we only make things worse. Every time in my life when God had a significant next phase in store for me, I went through a wilderness experience first. What are we supposed to do in the wilderness experience? The psalmist offers a clue:

> He says, "Be still, and know that I am God;
> I will be exalted among the nations,
> I will be exalted in the earth."
> Psalm 46:10

In the wilderness, we cannot be self-sufficient. We cannot be independent. In the wilderness, it becomes obvious that without God our situation is hopeless. Then, when we feel most hopeless, God starts performing miracles, like the parting of the Red Sea, bringing water from rocks, and dropping manna from heaven.

A wilderness experience puts our own efforts into perspective. We generally need to quit striving so we can overcome the illusion that success is related to our much activity. Each of my seasons in the wilderness followed a time when there was much activity and the appearance of great success. In the wilderness experiences, I learned that most of the heavy lifting in life is done by God, and we are allowed to do a portion as we cooperate with Him. In the wilderness, God has also showed me that one blow struck at the right time will have more impact than hundreds or even thousands of activities. That's a good lesson for us to learn if we are to ever be like Jesus.

Jesus began His earthly ministry at age 30, and in three years of ministry, He was never in a hurry. He understood that following God's plan didn't always require much activity or for us to be in a hurry. The key was to do what God told Him to do when God told Him to do it.

Humility and Testing

What does the wilderness do for us? First, we are humbled. In his book, *Moses*, Chuck Swindoll offers a number of insights on humility. In the wilderness, for instance, God breaks us of our lust for recognition. How? One way is by isolation. This is always part of a wilderness experience.[12] During this time, we may feel like God has forgotten us or has left us behind. Opportunities seem to pass us by, and we think we'll never get out of this place.[13] But this is just our emotions playing tricks on us. We cannot make wise decisions relying on our emotions because Satan will try to deceive us through our feelings. But here's what God is really doing during this time: "He encircles us. He cares for us. He guards us as the pupil of his eye. And finally, he guides us."[14] Everything seems out of control when, in fact, God is very much in control. God may seem distant and uncaring, but He is caring for you more

12 Charles R. Swindoll, *Moses: A Man of Selfless Dedication* (Nashville: Thomas Nelson, 2009), 75.
13 Ibid.
14 Ibid., 75-76.

than any other time in life—just like you guard the pupil of your eye when any object tries to get in it!

Why must we go through this experience?

> *"You shall remember all the way which the Lord your*
> *God has led you in the wilderness these forty years,*
> *that He might humble you, testing you,*
> *to know what was in your heart whether you would*
> *keep his commands or not."*
> Deuteronomy 8:2 (NASB)

Humility makes us moldable and teachable by God.

God's second purpose for the wilderness is to test us to know what's in our hearts. But is it really a test so that *God* can see what's in our hearts? No. God already knows what's there. He knows everything. The test is so that *we* will know what's in our hearts. When we have been tested severely and found faithful, then we can move forward in confidence that we will be obedient to God's plan.

I should warn you here, from personal experience, that we can go through more than one wilderness experience. In fact, we keep going through wilderness experiences until we learn all that God wants to teach us, and until we are prepared to do what God wants us to do. I should also tell you that each wilderness experience tends to be harder than the last. If we don't learn from the present test, we will have to repeat it with more severity.

We seem to think the Christian life should get easier as we mature and pass certain tests. Yet think of it this way: if you were pursuing a doctorate degree, you would notice that the tests get increasingly harder. And you wouldn't expect it to be any other way, would you? The same is true in the Christian walk. God keeps growing us to the next level. Therefore, the tests have to get harder. Again, Chuck Swindoll offers an insightful observation about people who have "been there":

> You can always tell when you have met individuals refined by God in the wilderness. They are some of the most secure, genuinely humble, gracious, honest individuals one can imagine. It took the desert experience to do that.[15]

Personal Experience

One of my most significant wilderness experiences began in 1997 and continued for several years. That was the year the federal government began an investigation of the business where I worked. It was a time of great challenge and testing.

The company had changed leadership three years earlier, and my sense of identity, self-worth, and security were all being challenged during this time. Being honest has always been an important virtue to me. Yet I was dealing with some people—and I should emphasize *some* federal agents—who had a particular vision of what had happened at the company and who had an idea of what they wanted me to say about events and people. When I didn't say what they wanted to hear, some were pretty angry with me. It's fairly uncomfortable

---

15 Ibid., 79.

knowing you are right but to have people with subpoena power and the power of the federal government mad at you.

That situation colored everything. If I wasn't preparing for discussions with officials or doing interviews with them, it seemed like I was preparing for and giving depositions with civil lawyers. All this went on while I was trying to do the job of President of Physician Services, which was a completely new experience for me. It seemed that everything I knew was either being challenged or changing. Everything that made me feel secure had changed. My sense of self-esteem was gone, and every day was just plain hard. It seemed like I was merely surviving from one day to the next. There were moments in some days that I even found it hard to breathe, like an elephant was sitting on my chest. During this time, though, God was faithful in His assurance. A particular Scripture verse kept coming to me from different sources— Jeremiah 29:11:

> *"For I know the plans I have for you," declares the*
> *LORD, "plans to prosper you and not to harm you,*
> *plans to give you hope and a future"*
> Jeremiah 29:11

Little did I know that God was preparing me for a future far better than I could have imagined. But I was being tested. My integrity and honesty were tested. My endurance was tested. My patience was tested. Finally, my faith was tested. Chuck Swindoll likes to point out that God doesn't care about your comfort nearly as much as He cares about your character, and as much as I hated the discomfort, it certainly did a work to develop my character.

After several years of the federal investigation and settling civil lawsuits, I thought the difficulties were finally over for me. Then one day I had some tests run, and a doctor told me, "This is not what you want to hear, but you have colon cancer."

What I remember so distinctly about that time is how little emotion I had. First, I was not scared at all. And when I say that I had *no* fear, I literally had no fear. I wasn't upset. I wasn't angry. My thought was, *Okay, God, what's next?* I never for a moment thought God had brought me through all that had just happened to let me die of colon cancer. And sure enough, the surgery and recovery both went well. The only thing I struggled with was the length of my chemotherapy treatment. Through all of it, though, I was calmer, more patient, and less fearful than I had been in my life. So what do I attribute this to? My response is what a significant trip in the wilderness experience will do.

How It Feels

In the wilderness experience, everything we counted on for our sense of identity, control, and normalcy is taken from us. It feels unfair and unnecessary, and worst of all, we think it will never end. We think we've learned all that God wants to teach us because we've cried out many times with what we think is a sincere heart, and yet the testing continues. The amount of time it takes seems totally unreasonable. We think we can't stand it any longer, and then it goes on some more. I've had this experience and watched others as they've gone through the same.

One godly man I know went through an extended wilderness experience during which he humbled himself. He begged for relief. Yet it went on and on. Throughout, however, there were clear evidences of divine intervention. The man caught glimpses of God's grace and mercy, and then finally a breakthrough happened, and he began to come out.

Chuck Swindoll points out the importance of responding correctly to the wilderness season: "Common responses to this season are I don't need it, I'm tired of it, and finally, if we are wise, I accept it."[16]

Why do we need to accept it? Because God hasn't forgotten us. If you find yourself in a situation that seems terribly unfair, don't give up. We have the promise of Jeremiah 29:11: "For I know the plans I have for you...plans to prosper you and not to harm you, plans to give you hope and a future." We are often quick to claim this promise but even quicker to forget it.

During the wilderness experience, we become more aware of our dependence on God than any other time life. In the wilderness, it's critical that your prayer life be deep and vibrant. Pray for God's daily provision. Pray for miracles. Offer up prayers of gratitude for God's daily provision and His miracles. It's hard for me to imagine anyone surviving the wilderness experience without a solid prayer life.

---

16 Ibid.

Summary

What is the Wilderness like?

It's hard. It's uncomfortable. It's humiliating. And it seems to go on forever.

What is God's purpose?

To humble you and test what is in your heart to see if you will obey Him. The test is not so that God will know, but so that you will know what's in your heart.

What is the proper response?

Humble yourself, and learn all that God wants to teach you during this time. Start getting excited about what God has for you next!

Go Deeper

1. Has God stripped away from you everything you used to find comfort or confidence in?

2. Is God humbling you?

3. Do you feel stretched and tested? If so, in what areas?

THE SEASON OF SOLITUDE

······································

We are such busy creatures. We see no reason for quietness and solitude. But God does. Often we make it hard for ourselves to receive all that God wants to give us at these times.

Chapter 14

The scripture that reminds me of the season of solitude is "be still and know that I am God" (Psalm 46:10), but it seems to be nothing like the world we live in. I've never seen a culture where people are so busy, go so hard and fast, long for rest, but refuse to rest when opportunities come. (While I discuss this as a separate season, Solitude can be a part of any of the other seasons, such as the Wilderness or Chastisement.)

God knew we would be busy, anxious creatures. That's one reason He doesn't just *allow* us to rest but *commands* us to rest. Resting every seventh day is a direct command of God, and He also built many other seasons of feasting and rest into the Old Testament patterns of life. According to Scripture, even God rested. The Bible says He created for six days and then rested on the seventh. God sees the value of rest, but apparently we don't. He has to convince us to rest, as reflected in the famous twenty-third Psalm: "He makes me lie down in green pastures."

Notice the verse says that God *makes* me lie down. Sheep are anxious, fearful creatures and have a tendency to always be active. That's why the shepherd has to make the sheep lie down and rest. God is the same way with us. He makes us rest. But why? Here are a few of the reasons I've come up with:

- He knows there's a period ahead that will be

more intense, and we need rest, reflection, and renewed spiritual strength to face it;

- He knows that we are more tired than we realize and that we really need to rest to get recharged and energized spiritually;

- He wants us to realize that it doesn't all depend on us.

God wants to do mighty works in and through us, and while we have to cooperate and work hard at times ourselves (He feeds the birds, but they also have to scratch), God is working through us. Anytime I look back, I see that He's always done the heavy lifting.

Elijah

God led Elijah to live beside a stream for three years. He gave him water during the drought and food by ravens during a season of starvation for many. After that, He led Elijah to the city where he would ask a poor widow to take her last bit of flour and make a cake for him. And what was the purpose of this season of solitude? As I said earlier, it was to prepare him in every way—especially spiritually—to face an evil queen and her 400 prophets. When the time came, Elijah knew exactly what to do:

Then Elijah commanded them,
"Seize the prophets of Baal. Don't let anyone get away!"
They seized them, and Elijah had them brought down

to the Kishon Valley and slaughtered there.
1 Kings 18:40

Downtime

I've been through two major seasons of solitude. One was at the end of one of my major wilderness experiences. At the time I thought, *Finally life is back to normal.* Then came my bout with cancer.

After my surgery, I couldn't go back to work for two weeks and then had to phase back into a regular schedule. I went from a season during which my schedule had been full every day for years to a period of serious downtime. I read my Bible, prayed, read books, sat, and reflected. I had a lot of time to think, to get centered, and to get back to my core. And why did God give me this time? Because He knew in my next major assignment I would need this "stored up" time of reflection and rest. I would need to have my head and priorities straight. My "joint assignment" of leading HCA's physician services while serving the executive pastor role at my church would take all that was within me spiritually, emotionally, psychologically, and intellectually. It was also exactly what I needed to be doing.

I love studying and working with people, and I love analyzing, understanding, and leading organizations. A large church is one of the biggest challenges in both areas I have ever experienced. That assignment would take three years, and before it was over, I drew on all that I had learned about people, organizations, and other experiences in my many seasons. I clearly would not have been ready for this experience had it not been for the wilderness experience which built my confidence in God, not in myself, and my season of solitude which gave me the opportunity to rest, study, reflect, and get centered again.

Jesus

Solitary seasons in Jesus' life came just before powerful movements of God for Kingdom work. Jesus spent the night alone in prayer before He chose His disciples. He won His ultimate spiritual battle alone with God in the Garden of Gethsemane. The victory was displayed on the cross and in the resurrection. Likely the greatest successes in your spiritual life, too, will come after seasons of solitude.

At daybreak, Jesus went out to a solitary place.
The people were looking for him and when they came
to where he was, they tried to keep him from leaving
them.
Luke 4:42

But Jesus often withdrew to lonely places and prayed.
Luke 5:16

Alone Again

Another major season of solitude occurred for me in 2010. At God's leading, I had resigned from my job as President of Physician Services at HCA. My last three years there had been quite productive as the depth and breadth of the function expanded. My calendar was full, and I had drifted back into thinking that much activity was important. I thought the preparation and the transition from the corporate world to starting my own foundation to live out my calling of developing leaders would similarly result in immediate productivity and a full calendar. Yet the exact opposite happened. I was just as surprised as Abraham probably was when God called him to the Promised Land to be the father of a nation but led him to a desert where there was a famine in progress.

Paul

After his Damascus Road conversion and his time in Jerusalem with Ananias, the Apostle Paul entered a significant season of solitude. God led him to a place of solitude where he spent three years. Paul says that he was trained by Christ Himself during this time:

But when God, who set me apart from my mother's womb and called me by his grace, was pleased to reveal his Son in me so that I might preach him among the Gentiles, my immediate response was not to consult any human being. I did not go up to Jerusalem to see those who were apostles before I was, but I went into Arabia. Later I returned to Damascus. Then after three years, I went up to Jerusalem to get acquainted with Cephas and stayed with him fifteen days. I saw none of the other apostles— only James, the Lord's brother. I assure you before God that what I am writing you is no lie.

Then I went to Syria and Cilicia.
I was personally unknown to the churches of Judea
that are in Christ. They only heard the report:
"The man who formerly persecuted us is now
preaching the faith he once tried to destroy."
And they praised God because of me.
Galatians 1:15-24

We tend to read through Scripture so quickly that we think Paul was converted and then went immediately to the mission field. This three years, though, was critical for Paul in finding his spiritual center, learning from Christ, and being ready to enter ministry as a missionary.

Solitude is the time for your prayer life to flourish. You have plenty of time in this season not only to talk to God but to listen deeply to what He's telling you in your spirit. Be sure to drink it all in.

Summary

What is Solitude like?

Extremely lonely.

What is God's purpose?

To get you to focus on Him only in order to prepare you for a season of productive service.

What is the proper response?

Be quiet and still and learn all God wants to teach you. Enjoy the quiet! It won't last that long, and you need it.

Go Deeper

1. Has God isolated you for a season? For how long?

2. What are you doing with your time?

3. Are you getting closer to God or further from Him?

*L*AMENT

••••••••••••••••••••••

Sometimes we hurt so bad that all we can do is cry. As long as we cry out to God, our tears can serve some purpose. Pain without purpose is a taste of HELL.

Chapter 15

Although the season of lament can be part of other seasons, I think it helps to look at it separately. There can be many causes for Lament: loss of a loved one, divorce, chronic illness, disability, business or financial loss. What makes it a season is the depth and length of our hurt.

> *"How long, O Jehovah? Will you forget me forever?*
> *How long will you hide your face from me?"*
> Psalms 13:1

From this psalm we can draw several conclusions:

- David wanted to sense God's presence but couldn't.

- He really desired to feel God near him. Instead, he felt abandoned.

- Since he couldn't sense God's presence, he assumed God had left him. Though not true, it's definitely the way he felt.

What can we learn from David's concerns? A key takeaway is that our emotions will deceive us. They are not reliable for determining reality, especially spiritual reality. God did not leave David and never would, no matter how he felt.

Even Jesus felt this way on the cross when He cried out, "My God, My God, why have You forsaken Me?" When He took on the sins of the world, that sin made Him feel separated from God's presence. God did not abandon Him or quit loving Him even for a second, but Jesus didn't sense that when *our* sins were laid on Him. It made Him feel separated from God.

So what is God doing with us during these times? They seem so deep and dark that some have referred to the season of lament as the "dark night of the soul." This is when God is molding us into the image of Christ. It's a refining time. One overwhelming characteristic of this period is that it seems to go on and on—longer than is reasonable or necessary to us. But what God does, He does extremely well, and He continues the refining.

I'm reminded of what the Apostle Paul says to the Corinthian Christians:

> *But we have this treasure in jars of clay to show that*
> *this all-surpassing power is from God and not from us.*
> *We are hard pressed on every side, but not crushed;*
> *perplexed, but not in despair; persecuted, but not*
> *abandoned; struck down, but not destroyed.*
> *We always carry around in our body the death of Jesus,*
> *so that the life of Jesus may also be revealed in our body.*
> *For we who are alive are always being given over*
> *to death for Jesus' sake, so that his life may also be*
> *revealed in our mortal body. So then, death is at work in*
> *us, but life is at work in you.*
> 2 Corinthians 4:7-12

Saints from Abraham to Esther to David to Paul went through this season. Everyone through whom God is going to do something significant goes through a time of lament. It is refinement for the mighty things God has next in that person's life.

What is the proper response to these times? David offers the answer at the end of Psalm 13:

> *But I trusted in your steadfast love;*
> *my heart shall rejoice in your salvation.*
> *I will sing to the LORD,*
> *because he has dealt bountifully with me.*
> Psalm 13:5-6

Though David started out lamenting, he ends by trusting God and rejoicing in Him. David realized something that we all need to realize:

God is not predictable, but He is consistent. We don't know how God is going to shape our lives, but we know He is. We don't know how He is going to deliver us, but we know He will.[17]

During Lament, we must be completely vulnerable and honest—from the depth of our souls—in prayer. God already knows how we feel and why. We don't need to tell Him what is going on to make sure He has the information. We need to cry out to Him, so that we leave our pain with Him and let His Spirit begin to heal us. The situations causing our

---

17 Quote attributed to Aaron Bryant.

lament may not go away. The chronic illness may remain. The loved one who has died will not return. But you will experience renewed spiritual strength that puts your focus on God and your trust in Him, even for the next breath you take. We endure or get through this season because we realize that God never abandons us.

Mary

If anyone ever had a season of lament, I expect it was Mary, the mother of Jesus. Imagine the great promises she had received and what she experienced as Jesus' mother while He grew up. Then imagine standing at the cross and seeing her Son crucified. The cry from her soul had to be as deep as what anybody had ever experienced. But after her time of lament, she saw her Son in all His resurrected glory! The season of lament always passes!

Summary

....

What is the season of Lament like?

It's painful. It seems to continue without purpose.

What is God doing?

He seems to be doing nothing. But He strengthens you through His Spirit.

What is the proper response?

Cast all your cares on Him! Cry your eyes out. Then trust Him to dry your tears

Go Deeper

1. Is something breaking your heart right now?

2. What are you doing with it?

3. Are you taking it to God and trusting Him with it?

THE *B*ACKSLIDING *S*EASON

The backslider is a miserable soul! People in this season are not fully committed in their walk with God. They feel cold toward Him, like He is absent. Still, they aren't completely accepted by people of this world. Although they can sin like a pagan, they cannot enjoy it like a pagan. The backslider is a person without a people.

When I kept silent, my bones wasted away
through my groaning all day long. For day and night
your hand was heavy on me; my strength was sapped
as in the heat of summer. Then I acknowledged my
sin to you and did not cover up my iniquity.
I said, "I will confess my transgressions to the Lord."
And you forgave the guilt of my sin.
Psalm 32:3-5

Chapter 16

When I was a boy, we commonly had one- to two-week revivals in the old country churches, and I don't think my family ever missed a single night. These events are ingrained in my mind, and over time, I've given a lot of thought to why we held so many revivals.

One of the primary reasons for revivals was to get church members reinvigorated and to appeal to backsliders. And what is a backslider? It is someone who had been serious about his or her walk with Christ but has fallen back into a pattern of worldliness and sin. While I think "backslider" captures the essence of what this season is about, I could have called it the season of the double-minded, using the words from James:

If any of you lacks wisdom, you should ask God,
who gives generously to all without finding fault, and
it will be given to you. But when you ask,
you must believe and not doubt,
because the one who doubts is like a wave of the sea,
blown and tossed by the wind.
That person should not expect to receive anything
from the Lord. Such a person is
double-minded *and unstable in all they do.*
James 1:5-8 (emphasis mine)

To be double-minded means that we go back and forth from having God as our priority to having self and the world as our priority. Scripture says the double-minded person should not expect anything from God. This, in part, explains the misery of the double-minded or backslidden person.

A woman I know summed this up quite well, speaking about her sister. She said, "The problem is my sister has just enough spirituality to make her miserable. God is not a priority, but she is not comfortable living in sin."

Sometimes it's hard to distinguish children of the dark versus light. Their actions, attitudes, and behavior can seem exactly the same. However, if you get close enough and know them well enough, you can discern a difference. The unsaved person can walk deeper and deeper in sin and his or her conscience is consistently deadened to the point that sin no longer bothers such a person. For true believers, though, who have the Spirit of Christ living in them, they can do horrible things—think of King David and his adultery with Bathsheba and the murder of her husband—and they can continue in sin so that their consciences are dulled to some degree. What they cannot get away from is the constant conviction of the Holy Spirit drawing them back toward repentance. In other words, backslidden believers can sin, but they cannot experience the same unhindered enjoyment of sin that a lost person can. Let's look at Psalm 51 to see David's prayer of repentance because of his misery over the sin that he committed:

Wash away all my iniquity and cleanse
me from my sin.

For I know my transgressions,
and my sin is always before me.
Psalm 51:2-3

When I kept silent, my bones wasted away
through my groaning all day long. For day and night
your hand was heavy on me; my strength was sapped
as in the heat of summer. Then I acknowledged my
sin to you and did not cover up my iniquity.
I said, "I will confess my transgressions to the Lord."
And you forgave the guilt of my sin.
Psalm 32:3-5

After reading the book *Deeper Experiences of Famous Christians*—which details biographies of a number of saints from the last three centuries—I recognized a couple of things the Christians in the book had in common. They all had a genuine conversion experience that forever removed the penalty of sin from their lives. Then they entered a season of going back to some sinful habits of their old, pre-converted lives. They were backslidden for a season.

I was amazed as I read about these great saints of the past who had significant conversion experiences and really felt a deep passion for God and His ways. Then each one of them returned to some sinful practice of the pre-conversion life. Some even went through seasons of sin darker and more serious than in their pre-conversion lives. They also experienced a season of discipline before getting back on the path to God. Each of them eventually repented, returned to following God, and became available for God to do something significant with them.

I need to be clear here and say that it is not possible for someone born of the Spirit of God to become unborn. We are all sinners! Some of us are lost sinners, and some are saved sinners. Saved sinners can go back to their old ways but cannot enjoy sin like a lost person. The Spirit of God will always convict them until they repent or are taken to heaven.

You can sin just like an unconverted person, but you can never enjoy the sin as they do because of the work of the Holy Spirit in your life. Your life is quite miserable when you walk in this season. When King David confessed his sins, he said:

> *For I know my transgressions,*
> *and my sin is always before me.*
> Psalms 51:3

Here was a man that God Himself had said was a man after His own heart. Yet David committed grievous sins. It was his season of backsliding. David let fear replace his faith in the God who told him that he would be the king of Israel. He went backward and forgot the promises of God. In order to walk down the backslidden path, we have to forget or ignore the many beautiful promises God makes in Scripture.

At one point, David became more comfortable with the enemy of God's people—the Philistines—than he was with God's people:

> *So he pretended to be insane in their presence;*
> *and while he was in their hands he acted like a madman,*

making marks on the doors of the gate and letting saliva
run down his beard.
1 Samuel 21:13

The same is true with us when we are backslidden. The first thing we do is to stop fellowshipping with other believers. We quit going to church. We quit spending time with Christian friends. We quit reading our Bible. We stop praying. We spend more time with unbelievers because we are more comfortable with them than God's people. But in the story of David, Scripture shows what happens next:

So Achish called David and said to him,
"As surely as the Lord lives, you have been reliable,
and I would be pleased to have you serve with me in
the army. From the day you came to me until
today, I have found no fault in you, but the rulers
don't approve of you."
1 Samuel 29:6

David wasn't really one of the pagan king's people. They rejected him. But he didn't feel at home with God's people, either. What a miserable state—a man without a people. That's what a true backslider is like.

The prayer life of a backslidden Christian is almost nonexistent. Rather than looking to God for solutions, we look to self or others. David had temporarily lost his faith in God. After all, why would he go to God in prayer when he thought God couldn't or wouldn't help him? That's how we all are when we are in a backslidden condition.

Summary

What is the Backsliding season like?

It's miserable. We are not fully devoted to Christ but cannot enjoy sinning like pagans. "Now the spirit of the Lord had departed from Saul, and an evil spirit from the Lord tormented him" (1 Samuel 16:14).

What is the purpose of the Backsliding season?

It serves no real purpose in the kingdom of God and is only a distraction from God's work of grace in our lives. It will bring about God's discipline until we return to Him or until we die. Scriptures talk about those who leave this life early because of their unrepentant sin (1 John 5:16b).

What should be our response to God in this season?

Quick and complete repentance and returning to God and His ways.

Go Deeper

1. Has your relationship with God grown cold?

2. Have you returned to the sins of your pre-converted life?

3. Are you more comfortable with Christians or with non-Christians?

4. Are you growing in your faith?

ENDURANCE

People who can't endure great trials may not be committed to the course and do not make the best soldiers in a fight. Jesus commands us to endure to build our faith and character.

Consider it pure joy, my brothers and sisters,
whenever you face trials of many kinds,
because you know that the testing of your faith
produces perseverance
James 1:2-3

Blessed is the one who perseveres under trial because,
having stood the test, that person will receive the
crown of life that the Lord has promised to those who
love him.
James 1:12

To those who by persistence in doing good seek glory,
honor and immortality, He will give eternal life.
Romans 2:7

Chapter 17

The Apostle James knew a great deal about suffering and endurance, and so did the Apostle Paul. Paul explained how much he suffered for the kingdom:

Five times I received from the Jews the forty lashes
minus one. Three times I was beaten with rods,
once I was pelted with stones, three times
I was shipwrecked, I spent a night and a day in the
open sea, I have been constantly on the move.
I have been in danger from rivers, in danger from
bandits, in danger from my fellow Jews, in danger
from Gentiles; in danger in the city, in danger in the
country, in danger at sea; and in danger from false be-
lievers. I have labored and toiled and have often gone
without sleep; I have known hunger and thirst and
have often gone without food; I have been cold and
naked. Besides everything else, I face daily the
pressure of my concern for all the churches.
Who is weak, and I do not feel weak?
Who is led into sin, and I do not inwardly burn?
2 Corinthians 11:24-29

And look at what Job had to endure:

One day when Job's sons and daughters were feasting
and drinking wine at the oldest brother's house, a

> messenger came to Job and said, "The oxen were
> plowing and the donkeys were grazing nearby,
> and the Sabeans attacked and made off with them.
> They put the servants to the sword,
> and I am the only one who has escaped to tell you!"
> While he was still speaking, another messenger came
> and said, "The fire of God fell from the heavens and
> burned up the sheep and the servants, and I am the
> only one who has escaped to tell you!"
> While he was still speaking, another messenger came
> and said, "The Chaldeans formed three raiding parties
> and swept down on your camels and made off with
> them. They put the servants to the sword, and I am
> the only one who has escaped to tell you!"
> While he was still speaking, yet another messenger
> came and said, "Your sons and daughters were
> feasting and drinking wine at the oldest brother's
> house, when suddenly a mighty wind swept in from
> the desert and struck the four corners of the house.
> It collapsed on them and they are dead, and I am the
> only one who has escaped to tell you!"
> Job 1:13-19

The purpose of our trials is not to break us but to make us. As I said earlier, Chuck Swindoll often points out that "God is more interested in developing your character than providing for your comfort," and that certainly applies during the season of endurance. It's not that God doesn't care about your comfort. He just knows what is best for you.

Trials make you strong. The Apostle Paul talked about how he was pressured from all sides but grew stronger inside.

Scripture makes it clear that those belonging to God are to endure:

> *But the one who stands firm to the end will be saved.*
> Matthew 24:13

There is a clear line connecting those who are committed and endure to those who are saved. So are we saved because of our endurance? No. We endure because Christ has saved us! We have the Spirit of God within, helping us to endure.

Early in their walk with Jesus, the first apostles were safe, secure, and relatively comfortable. Even the Apostle Paul was safe, secure, and comfortable. It was in the late stages of their maturity and final chapter of life when they were called to endure great sufferings for the sake of Christ—often to the point of dying for the gospel.

God's Purpose in Pain

Christians have difficulty with some scriptures teaching about how God deals with His people. One problem has to do with the amount of pain involved in some of the seasons. Americans don't have an adequate theology of pain. Generally, we do not see purpose in pain as God does:

> *[W]e also glory in our sufferings,*
> *because we know that suffering produces perseverance;*
> *perseverance, character; and character, hope.*
> Romans 5:3-4

Our flawed theology is not new. It was very much alive in Jesus' day, and that's why He told the story of Lazarus and the rich man. Jesus paints a great contrast between the earthly life of these two men. One was wealthy and lacked for nothing. People of that day believed wealth and health was a sign of God's blessing. Therefore, they naturally assumed the rich man was favored by God. In contrast, they considered sickness to be a result of some sin in the person's life. It was a sign of God's displeasure with that person. So in His story, Jesus describes in detail the physical condition of Lazarus. He was broke and begging at the rich man's gate. His body was covered with painful sores. He was so weak that he couldn't even shoo the dogs away. They licked his open sores.

For Jesus' listeners, the surprise ending came when Jesus described the eternal state of the two men. The rich man did not have God's favor. He ended up tormented in hell. Here's the whole story:

*There was a rich man who was dressed in purple
and fine linen and lived in luxury every day.
At his gate was laid a beggar named Lazarus, covered
with sores and longing to eat what fell from the rich
man's table. Even the dogs came and licked his sores.
The time came when the beggar died and the angels
carried him to Abraham's side.
The rich man also died and was buried.
In Hades, where he was in torment,
he looked up and saw Abraham far away, with
Lazarus by his side. So he called to him,
"Father Abraham, have pity on me and send Lazarus*

to dip the tip of his finger in water and cool my
tongue, because I am in agony in this fire."
But Abraham replied, "Son, remember that in your
lifetime you received your good things, while Lazarus
received bad things, but now he is comforted here and
you are in agony. And besides all this, between us and
you a great chasm has been set in place, so that those
who want to go from here to you cannot,
nor can anyone cross over from there to us."
Luke 16:19-26

Lazarus had God's favor and was to spend eternity in heaven and be comforted.

Suffering is not just for those who follow Christ. God Himself chose to suffer by sending His only Son to the cross. Jesus, too, suffered, but for what purpose? To show His love for us. Jesus chose to suffer on the cross rather than call down angels to deliver Him.

What if God had chosen not to suffer? What if Jesus had chosen not to suffer? We would be lost and on our way to hell. And what happens if we choose not to suffer? It means that people we know will be lost and on their way to hell because our suffering may be part of God's plan for reaching them.

Many places in Scripture remind us that we must be willing to suffer for Christ. The apostles even praised God for being considered worthy of suffering for Christ. Which brings me to another question: if Christ suffered to show His love for us, then why are we called to suffer for Jesus? To show our love for Him.

*Blessed is the one who perseveres under trial because,
having stood the test, that person will receive the
crown of life that the Lord has promised to
those who love him.*
James 1:12

Most people are not surprised that continued obedience is part of the proper response to suffering, but they are surprised that praise is part of the proper response. The Apostle James said to consider it all joy when we encounter various trials. And look at how Peter and some of the other apostles responded after being beaten and put in prison for their faith:

*The apostles left the Sanhedrin,
rejoicing because they had been counted worthy
of suffering disgrace for the Name.*
Acts 5:41

While I have written about this as a specific season in the Christian's life, there is a degree to which Endurance is an overarching season for a Christian's whole walk. The same can be said of joy and peace. There are particular seasons when we experience an abundance of joy and peace. However, these are an overarching and ongoing part of every Spirit-led Christian's life. A strong prayer life is critical to the season of Endurance because no one can get through it without relying on God through continued prayer.

Summary
....

What is the season of Endurance like?

It tests and tries you from all angles. It's not just painful but very stressful.

What is the purpose of the season?

To make you strong so that you can withstand anything for the sake of Christ.

What is the proper response?

Continued obedience, praise, and prayer.

Go Deeper

1. Are you struggling to make it spiritually?

2. What pressures do you feel the most?

3. Is your prayer life strong and consistent?

4. Are your Christian friends encouraging you?

GRATITUDE

. . . .

*God inhabits the praises of His people.
He loves our praises, and gratitude lifts our
countenance.*

*Always giving thanks to God the Father
for everything, in the name of our Lord Jesus Christ.*
Ephesians 5:20

*Do not be anxious about anything,
but in every situation, by prayer and petition,
with thanksgiving, present your requests to God.*
Philippians 4:6

Chapter 18

While gratitude is another overarching season for all of the Christian life, there are some periods in which this seems more natural than others. When we are in the faith-building stage of life and God is blessing us, for instance, praise feels very natural. When God leads us out of the wilderness experience, we are especially grateful. When the pruning or discipline stops, we appreciate the relief. No matter what the situation, though, the key reason we can always give thanks is that God is at work in us:

> *Now to him who is able to do immeasurably more*
> *than all we ask or imagine, according to his power*
> *that is at work within us,*
> Ephesians 3:20

> *Being confident of this, that he who began a*
> *good work in you will carry it on to completion until*
> *the day of Christ Jesus.*
> Philippians 1:6

What may seem counterintuitive is having gratitude during some of the tough seasons. We should be thankful to God even during the wilderness experience, during a season of discipline, during a season of solitude, and during our season of trials and endurance.

The Word says God inhabits the praises of His people, so when God gave Jehoshaphat and the children of Israel a mighty victory, for instance, Scripture says that God began to slay the enemy after the children of Israel started their praise. God loves our praise—and always deserves it. In addition, it's good for us. Gratitude and praising God will do much to lift our own countenance.

Our prayer life clearly reveals whether or not we are in this season. On the one hand, we might focus on what we don't have and feel left out. If this continues, it can lead to despair. On the other hand, if we follow Scripture and give thanks in all things, our prayers will be filled with gratitude. The difference isn't in our circumstances but rather how we see them and how we choose to pray.

I have to make a confession: gratitude is not something I have typically been good at. I have had my extended moments of thanksgiving, like when certain major struggles passed in my life. However, my hardwiring and orientation tend to draw me to see what is not right rather than what is good. I tend to look at what I'm striving for rather than what God has already given me.

I have begun to pray continually for the joy and peace of God, and He has shown me that the key is daily expressing gratitude in prayer for all He has given me and done for me. As I do this, I begin to see the value of being thankful in all things. Gratitude will take you to a new place spiritually, and it will give you peace and joy like you've never experienced.

Summary

What does Gratitude feel like?
It's wonderful. We can't believe how blessed we are.

What is God's purpose in the season?
To bless us as we recognize His greatness.

What should be our response?
Praise!

Go Deeper

1. Are you thankful for what you have or resentful for what you don't have?

2. What have you sincerely thanked God for this week?

Sunset

....

We reap what we sow, often in this life, but always in the age to come. What are you sowing to create your Sunset season?

Now then, just as the Lord promised, he has kept me alive for forty-five years since the time he said this to Moses, while Israel moved about in the wilderness. So here I am today, eighty-five years old! I am still as strong today as the day Moses sent me out; I'm just as vigorous to go out to battle now as I was then. Now give me this hill country that the Lord promised me that day. You yourself heard then that the Anakites were there and their cities were large and fortified, but, the Lord helping me, I will drive them out just as he said.
Joshua 14:10-12

Chapter 19

This season could also be called the season of harvest. Several Old Testament saints experienced this special time—Job quickly comes to mind. After he had endured a season of significant testing, God blessed him in the latter part of his life more than the first part. He got to enjoy his children, grandchildren, and great-grandchildren. He had good friends and a good reputation. He had more than enough material goods. He lived in peace and enjoyed life.

Jacob, the father of the 12 tribes of Israel, also experienced this season. He had endured significant trials, primarily because of his own sin. However, he is finally reunited with his favorite son, Joseph, who had become second in command to the pharaoh of Egypt. And Jacob also sees his other sons grow up and take greater responsibility. They ended up living together in the most fertile section of Egypt, called the Land of Goshen, where all their needs were met. Here's the joyful summary of the story:

Then Jacob left Beersheba, and Israel's sons took their father Jacob and their children and their wives in the carts that Pharaoh had sent to transport him. So Jacob and all his offspring went to Egypt, taking with them their livestock and the possessions they had acquired in Canaan. Jacob brought with him

> *to Egypt his sons and grandsons and his daughters*
> *and granddaughters—all his offspring.*
> Genesis 46:5-7

The Israelites experienced this season when they settled in the Promised Land:

> *The Lord gave them rest on every side,*
> *just as he had sworn to their ancestors.*
> *Not one of their enemies withstood them;*
> *the Lord gave all their enemies into their hands.*
> Joshua 21:44

I must say that I yearn for this season in my own life. Yet I admit that I'm not sure how this works for the New Testament Christian. Scripture demonstrates this season very clearly in the lives of Old Testament saints and perhaps in a few New Testament saints. Yet I tend to think the New Testament era is different. Our world will become increasingly hostile to Christians, and we are called to endure. We may not experience the sunset season in our bodies.

Our prayer life should be especially strong during this season. As we look over God's times of provision and intervention during our lives, we should be filled with praise. As we endure whatever we may be called upon to do, we should go quickly to our Father in prayer.

Summary

What is the Sunset season like?

It is a time of peace for God's people.

What is God's purpose?

To build up people who are different than the world. His goal is that our lives would attract others to the faith.

What is an appropriate response?

Gratitude, praise, and right living before our lost neighbors.

Go Deeper

1. Do you sense spiritual contentment?

2. Do you see Kingdom fruit in your life?

3. What is God challenging you to do in this season of your life?

GLORIFICATION

....

We endure in these tired, worn-out bodies because we look forward to receiving our resurrection bodies when there will be no more pain or suffering, and we will live in eternal bliss.

Chapter 20

The season of glorification occurs after death. We live with Christ forever in a new, glorified body. This is what Stephen looked forward to when he had such peace during his death by stoning. It was what the Apostle Paul was looking for when he was struggled with whether it was better to go and be with Christ or to stay and continue his ministry.

Paul and Peter both knew some of the glories that were waiting for them:

> *I consider that our present sufferings are not worth*
> *comparing with the glory that will be revealed in us.*
> Romans 8:18

> *And the God of all grace, who called you to his eternal*
> *glory in Christ, after you have suffered a little while,*
> *will himself restore you and make you strong,*
> *firm and steadfast.*
> 1 Peter 5:10

Some people are not excited about the time of glorification. They envision people in white robes, floating on clouds and playing harps. And quite frankly, that imagery does seem boring. In reality, though, I believe heaven will be anything but boring! Whatever work God gave us to do on this earth that we are really good at and really enjoy, He will give more of it in heaven. Here's what Jesus had to say about that:

> *His master replied, "Well done, good and faithful*
> *servant! You have been faithful with a few things;*
> *I will put you in charge of many things.*
> *Come and share your master's happiness!"*
> Matthew 25:21

Heaven will be colorful—brighter, in fact, than anything we have experienced on earth. We read about the Garden of Eden in the Bible and picture paradise. But there will be a new heaven and new earth, and we will live in paradise, which will be as good as or better than the original.

Above all, we will live in the eternal presence of God our Father and Jesus Christ our Savior and Lord. We will be at perfect peace with Them and will perfectly experience Their love.

Summary

What is Glorification like?
Eternal bliss, joy, peace, and complete satisfaction.

What is God's purpose?
To show His lovingkindness and enjoy His children forever.

What should be our response?
Humble, awestruck, and eternal praise. Our communication with God will be constant in this season.

Go Deeper

1. Are you excited about heaven?

2. How do you envision heaven?

3. Do you think about heaven weekly or daily?

FINAL OBSERVATIONS

Chapter 21

The more I observe people in all walks of life—including ministry—the more I see that people tend to be hurting and confused. Some of this is because they don't understand which season of the soul they are in. Some people are angry when they should be glad. Some are content when they should be scared and making a change. Some are just trying to get by rather than enjoying all that God has for them in their spiritual walk. Many people are simply clueless. They're walking in the dark and have no idea where that will take them in eternity.

You have choices. You can walk in the dark. You can come into the light. You can walk into greater light during your life on this earth. Or you can stay in the gray and be miserable. Walking toward greater light in Christ has a price. There will be many trials as you are called on to endure. But all of us have this promise from the Apostle Peter and from Christ Himself:

> *And the God of all grace, who called you to his eternal*
> *glory in Christ, after you have suffered a little while,*
> *will himself restore you and make you strong,*
> *firm and steadfast.*
> 1 Peter 5:10

My prayer is that you will walk toward the light of Christ soon and not waste any time.

The Seasons

In Tennessee, where I live, we have four very distinct seasons. In the spring, you can enjoy the beauty of the dogwoods and redbud trees blooming. You can hike to waterfalls in some of our state parks. In summer, the trees are lush with green, and you can enjoy water sports in lakes across the state. In fall, the leaves are rich with color, especially in the mountains, where again you can enjoy hiking to the waterfalls. And in winter, you can enjoy snow skiing in the mountains.

As much as each season has to offer, however, if you try any of these activities out of season, your experience will be miserable. The same is true in your spiritual life. If you try to do things in the wrong season, you can be very unhappy very quickly.

The seasons I've described in this book correlate readily to seasons of the year. The unconverted person is in the winter season. They experience cold and dark. Life for the backslidden Christian is similar.

The Christian in the New Life season is like spring when there is new growth. The season of new faith is like summer when tremendous growth occurs. The Wilderness season is like the dry part of summer when heat and droughts are intense. The Sunset season and season of Glorification are like the harvest or fall season, and the season of Pruning is like late fall or early winter.

I encourage you to follow the instructions of the Apostle Paul and test yourself to see if you're truly in the faith. If you are, then please discover which post-conversion season you are in. If you are in a season where God is trying to build your faith, then ask for extraordinary things in accordance with His will and see the marvelous things He will do to increase your faith.

If you're in the Wilderness season, look for some miracle on the way, but endure the testing to discover what is really in your heart. Humble yourself quickly so that all pride is removed from your life, and the experience doesn't have to be prolonged. Also, be encouraged and excited that the next season God has for you will be like the Promised Land for the children of Israel. Eagerly anticipate it, and praise God in advance for it. But do not be fearful and disobedient. You can die in the wilderness. One whole generation of Israelites did.

If you're in a season of Lament, cry your eyes out. But turn to God in faith, knowing that this season will pass, and He will eventually bring joy to your life and His peace that we cannot fully understand but cannot deny.

If you're in a season of Endurance, then praise God because the testing of your faith produces endurance and patience and results in an everlasting crown of glory and honor! And remember the overarching seasons in which a Christian can live in joy and peace no matter what the specific season.

If you are in a season of Solitude, listen intently to God and slow down. Enjoy the rest and the quiet. Learn all that

God wants you to learn. You will need your solitude and rest for what is coming next in your life.

If you can identify the season you are in, then you can understand what God is doing and respond appropriately to prolong the good seasons and get the most Kingdom growth possible out of the tougher seasons. The one common thread in each season—no matter which one your soul finds itself in at the present time—is prayer. Prayer is a daily conversation with a loving heavenly Father who desires nothing more than to be with us each and every step of our journey toward eternity with Him. He eagerly awaits for us to seek His guidance and plan for our daily lives, and He alone knows exactly how each season of our souls brings us closer to Him and His perfect love for us.

Pray without ceasing. May God's peace be with you!

Notes

Notes

Notes

Notes

CPSIA information can be obtained
at www.ICGtesting.com
Printed in the USA
LVHW040549290819
629333LV00007B/35/P